THE HUNT FOR THE
LAST PUBLIC ENEMY

in

NORTHEASTERN OHIO

THE HUNT FOR THE
LAST PUBLIC ENEMY

in

NORTHEASTERN OHIO

Alvin "Creepy" Karpis and His Road to Alcatraz

JULIE A. THOMPSON
Foreword by Ian Craig

THE
History
PRESS

Published by The History Press
Charleston, SC
www.historypress.com

First published 2019

Manufactured in the United States

ISBN 9781467138208

Library of Congress Control Number: 2018966266

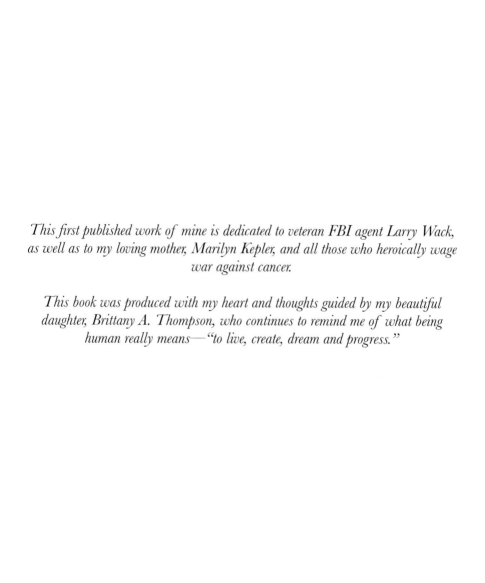

This first published work of mine is dedicated to veteran FBI agent Larry Wack, as well as to my loving mother, Marilyn Kepler, and all those who heroically wage war against cancer.

This book was produced with my heart and thoughts guided by my beautiful daughter, Brittany A. Thompson, who continues to remind me of what being human really means—"to live, create, dream and progress."

Alvin Karpis and J. Edgar Hoover, black-and-white illustration, 2018. *Willie "WD" Smith, Tennessee.*

THE THIEF: *Cops are cops! I'm sick and tired of everybody goin' green and startin' to shake when you talk about G-men. Feds—what are they, some sort of special creature? Sure they got the heat on me, but they haven't got me!*
—Alvin Karpis

THE JUSTICE: *The cure for crime is not the electric chair, but the high chair…*
—J. Edgar Hoover

─⟋∾∽⟍─

Per veteran FBI agent Larry Wack, in an e-mail dated March 6, 2018:

> *"Dear Sir:*
> *Is it true that you walked up to Alvin Karpis in the street*
> *and arrested him[?] I thought only agents arrest people.*
> *Thank you, Larry Wack*

I wanted to be a G-Man since the age of 13. At that age, and for years on and off, I used to write letters to JEH and the Bureau with all kinds of stupid questions about the gangster era and probably became a pain in the ass to them! Funny enough, I found a copy of my letter [above] to JEH in 1964 at the age of 14, pertaining to Karpis. This letter was in the Karpis file when I came across it.
Don't recall the Bureau's response or if they even responded at all. I was growing up in Willingboro, New Jersey, at the time."

CONTENTS

CONTENTS

FOREWORD

As students of U.S. Penitentiary–Alcatraz history, the path to a true understanding of the infamous prison leads directly to an exploration of the notorious "gangster era" in America. The study of this history also lends itself to the discovery of key figures who exemplified this dangerous period.

The government's response to this threat would result in a federal crackdown on organized crime, and it would also lead to the creation of America's first "super-maximum security" prison on Alcatraz Island in the San Francisco Bay. Any exploration of either the gangster era or the USP–Alcatraz will surely include the true-life story of a colorful yet sometimes deadly individual who dominated both the era and the inescapable federal prison. Alvin "Creepy" Karpis was this dangerous decade's final Public Enemy No. 1. He would ultimately serve the longest sentence ever served at USP–Alcatraz.

The following literary work clarifies the social structure of American culture during the late 1920s and early 1930s that gave rise to the emergence of timeless criminal folk heroes such as Al "Scarface" Capone, John Dillinger and the subject of this study, Alvin Karpis—kidnapper, bank robber, criminal mastermind, supposed murderer and fugitive extraordinaire.

This is a compelling story of daring criminal conspiracies, the period's public perception of lawlessness and the creation of the Federal Bureau of Investigation (FBI) and its perennial leader, J. Edgar Hoover. This work traces the emergence of this extremely cagey federal fugitive, his elusive path as leader of the Karpis-Barker Gang, his eventual capture and extreme incarcerations and better years after release from a life sentence.

The author of this close examination of this gangster-era icon, devoted historian Julie Thompson, has her roots firmly planted in northeastern Ohio. Julie, having been raised in the usually hushed village of Garrettsville, illuminates the importance of this unsuspecting setting for a brazen great train robbery with a never-before-attempted escape by airplane. Julie brings to light the mechanics of the gangster era's progression, illuminating the local histories of numerous American "breadbasket" Midwest states. The result had lasting national implications. Criminal associations included fellow infamous outlaws like George "Bugsy" Moran, George "Baby Face" Nelson, Kate "Ma" Barker and her boys (originally the Barker-Karpis Gang) and other nefarious connections made through these contacts.

Many of the Karpis-Barker Gang's crimes and hideouts inhabited many cities within Ohio, including Cleveland, Akron, the Canton area, Toledo and even "down south" in the secluded criminal hangout of Hot Springs, Arkansas.

New and gripping details emerge through this exploration on the planning and execution of Alvin Karpis's sensational federal crimes. Many titillating stories will enthrall readers featuring the roles of tommy guns, dynamite and creative getaway vehicles. Planes, trains and automobiles often played lively roles in Alvin's crimes, which makes this a worthwhile immersion into the daring details of these often-wild escapades.

Alvin Karpis was ultimately sentenced to a term of life in federal prison for his felonious kidnapping capers. Consequently, this life sentence imprisoned Karpis at Alcatraz for a record-setting twenty-six years (nearly), and he endured time on "the Rock" during all three decades of the institution's history.

Surprisingly, USP–Alcatraz was never at full capacity during its twenty-nine-year history. The U.S. Army had expanded the military prison to six hundred cells during the year 1912. When the Feds took over in 1934, they were never able to fill the prison. There just weren't enough "worst of the worst" criminals deserving of this level of containment or punishment.

Alvin Karpis was *not* one of these undeserving occupants. USP–Alcatraz had been extensively remodeled by the Bureau of Prisons from 1933 to 1934 with the goal of securely confining the gangster-criminal element of Karpis's kind. Alcatraz was designed to receive America's most dangerous who were now destined to serve long sentences in the new escape-proof federal prison.

In 1935, the drawn-out hunt for Karpis as a federal fugitive, spearheaded by Hoover and company, had been a constant source of embarrassment for the newly designated Federal Bureau of Investigation. As the top G-Man (or Government Man), Director J. Edgar Hoover was especially the target of criticism. The desperate and prolonged hunt for Karpis evolved into a source for exaggerated newspaper coverage and sensationalized pulp fiction.

The national press, as well as Hollywood movie production companies, became infatuated with the intriguing federal hunt for Karpis. This interest was coupled with the highly publicized prosecution of the sensational mob boss Al Capone, his transfer to USP–Alcatraz and the alluring mystique of "the Rock."

Immediately following the dramatic scene of the Garrettsville train robbery, numerous federal government agents were dispatched to the northeastern Ohio area to search for the elusive chief suspect, Alvin Karpis, and his numerous accomplices.

Throughout the past eight decades, this last great train heist in American history has been widely adopted as the backstory of Garrettsville local lore. This dramatic local history has been cemented in the choice for the athletic mascot of the area's high school, whose team is known as the James A. Garfield High School "Fighting G-Men" (author Julie Thompson's own alma mater).

Follow the extensive search for this last Public Enemy No. 1, stretching out over nearly three years to its culmination in the sensational capture by Hoover and his FBI. Also, discover the significant roles in this pursuit provided by law enforcement officials in Ohio, especially those efforts put forth by the U.S. Postal Service inspectors and the use of new investigative science, including latent fingerprinting techniques.

Ultimately, this published work, prepared with tireless dedication by Thompson, presents a fresh opportunity for an understanding of the complexities involved in the rise and fall of this atypical American gangster. This study also helps clarify the blurry legacy of J. Edgar Hoover as the famed nemesis and captor of Alvin Karpis.

The following is an invaluable discovery of the forces driving America's gangster era and a welcome work for historians and explorers of this timeless period. Enjoy getting to know Alvin "Creepy" Karpis, his daring criminal escapades, the amazing evasions of capture, his historic sentence on "the Rock" and his ultimate freedom. Thanks Julie for your exhaustive efforts and determination, and congratulations on the successful publication of this work. The legend of America's "Last Public Enemy No. 1," Alvin "Creepy" Karpis, lives on. Enjoy, and we'll hope to see you all on "the Rock"!

IAN CRAIG
Media Producer, NPS Volunteer,
Historical Interpretation, Alcatraz Island

ACKNOWLEDGEMENTS

T he single greatest cause of happiness is gratitude." And so I wish to express my joy in working with the many individuals whose talents and breadth of scholarship made this book possible. By far, the greatest assistance was provided by my dearest friend, Traci A. (Murphy) Falb, who over the course of the last year spent day and night guiding me through the research, editing and the writing of this work, my first published book. Traci provided her professional and candid expertise on the direction that this true crime story should take. So thank you, Trace! This work would not have been remotely possible without you.

Undoubtedly, the research that took shape and culminated in this true-crime story began at Hiram College. It is here at Hiram that James A. Garfield served as a college instructor and principal before he was elected the twentieth president of the United States and where this story first began as my senior capstone project. Without the support and guidance of my advisor, Vivien Sandlund, and the rest of the Hiram History Department, including Dr. Janet Pope and Donald Fleming, this story would likely never have been told. Additionally, I'd like to recognize my fellow Hiram College colleague and friend Maya J. Watkins, who graciously provided her well-honed technological and research abilities for this unique work. Maya also contributed to the editing of this book's manuscript.

I so humbly thank my husband and partner in this crime (pun intended), Lucian Thompson, and my esteemed uncle, William J. Gainer, for their steadfast support. Since the tender age of about nine years old, I can distinctly recall that my Uncle Bill was always a constant source of inspiration and someone I looked up to with the highest regard.

A special thanks to the following universities, libraries, societies and government agencies: Kent State University; University of Akron; Donna Stewart at Digital Production for the Michael Schwartz Library at Cleveland State University; Bowling Green and Ohio State Universities; Library of Congress; Department of Justice (FBI and the Bureau of Prisons); United States Postal Inspection Service; the National Archives located in Washington, D.C., Kansas City, Maryland, Seattle and San Bruno; the archivists at the Minnesota Historical Society; and the wealth of historical criminal information provided by the 1930s gangster files consolidated by St. Paul criminal historian and author Paul Maccabee.

Just as important to this work was the former president of the James A. Garfield Historical Society, Mrs. Kit Semplak of Garrettsville, Ohio. Kit was my very first contact regarding this unique and nearly untouched local/national true crime story. I'd also like to recognize award-winning author and Alcatraz historian Michael Esslinger for introducing me to the island through his unparalleled historical knowledge and his research of our country's most infamous former federal prison. A special thanks also to David Ward, Professor Emeritus of sociology at the University of Minnesota and author of a groundbreaking work on the federal prison system entitled *Alcatraz: The Gangster Years (2009)*. David provided me with specific insight into the wealth of information that he consolidated from his extensive research into the records of the FBI, the Bureau of Prisons and the federal parole records.

My appreciation also to criminal historian, author and illustrator Willie D. Smith for his exceptional work on this book's black-and-white illustration (see Mr. Smith's website at https://www.facebook.com/The-Barker-Karpis-Gang-An-American-Crime-Family-500446183452382). My sincere gratitude also to former Alcatraz inmates William G. Baker (author of the 2013 book *Alcatraz #1259*) and Robert "Bob" Schibline (AZ-1355), as well as former Alcatraz guards George DeVincenzi (author of the 2014 book *Murders on Alcatraz*) and Jim Albright (author of his 2008 memoirs *Last Guard Out*), all of whom offered written and verbal accounts of their unique experiences at Alcatraz. Additionally, Jared McDade, son of former FBI Special Agent Thomas McDade (1934–38), provided me with extensive and unique information focusing on his father's Bureau experiences and the lives of FBI agents during the 1930s. Also, many thanks to the Wadsworth Area Historical Society and its active volunteer, Duane Blubaugh, great-grandson of Wadsworth, Ohio chief of police

Tommy Lucas. Blubaugh added never-before-heard dialogue to this true crime story.

Throughout this effort, my progress was aided by dear friend and veteran FBI agent Larry Wack. Larry is also the author of the website Faded Glory: Dusty Roads of an FBI Era (see www.historicalgmen.squarespace. com). Larry guided me through this work, helping me to understand the perspective of the FBI through the eyes and ears of law enforcement. Also, critical to my success in completing this work was Ian Craig, a San Francisco media producer and renowned Alcatraz historical interpreter. Without Ian's guidance, knowledge, curiosity and unrivaled connections, this work would have been more difficult and the outcome diminished. Last, but certainly not least, much appreciation is extended to Susan Henry, the step-granddaughter of Dolores Delaney (Dee Higby). Sue provided a pivotal interview on the life of Dolores after her release from prison. A continuum of gratitude also goes to John Rodrigue, my commissioning editor at The History Press. John was unsurpassed in his patience and guidance.

My sincerest apologies if I inadvertently missed anyone, as so many contributed to this book's completion.

THE RISE IN NORTHEASTERN OHIO'S GANGSTER SIGHTINGS

The Roaring Twenties were hopeful with economic prosperity but witnessed the fierce and heated Eighteenth Amendment passed on January 17, 1920. Despite its intended purpose, forbidding the manufacture and sale of alcohol gave rise to a new age of rebels and lawlessness. As a result, rival gangs—many born of eastern and southern European immigrants and led by business-type racketeers like the powerful Al "Scarface" Capone and George "Bugsy" Moran—conducted their corrupt affairs in professional settings throughout Chicago and New York.

In an attempt to expand their territories, these racketeers became proficient in explosives, pistols and the "trench sweeper" of World War I—better known as the Thompson submachine gun.[1] Many of these gangsters, such as Capone, crossed state boundaries, preventing the local police from extending beyond their own borders to capture these savvy criminals.[2] This crime wave symbolized grave disorder in the American democracy, and many citizens would have been happy to declare martial law.

At the conclusion of the 1920s, the big-city business criminals such as Capone and his New York associate Charles "Lucky" Luciano were replaced with a new breed. Historian Storm Wallace noted that these lawbreakers lacked education and even the most basic work history, as many of them were the sons and daughters of farmers and hillbillies. These new "back-road bandits" were driven into their lawless pursuits by hunger and desperation. Most recklessly emulated the outlaws of the Old West, such as Jesse James and Billy the Kid. Unlike their urban predecessors, these Midwest bandits hardly lived the Hollywood lifestyle. At the height of Al Capone's power, he was illegally accumulating an annual income of about $30 million.[3] By comparison, the back-road bandit and eventual public enemy Alvin "Creepy" Karpis was netting just over $50,000 per year.[4]

The gun battles of the 1920s made way for the "Dirty Thirties," when the "American dream became the American nightmare."[5] From Indiana to Texas, these 1930s bandits were described as criminals who "moved swiftly and hit without mercy." In 1933, the country recorded twelve thousand murders, fifty thousand robberies and three thousand kidnappings. Like modern-day cowboys, these criminals utilized the Thompson submachine gun, capable of dispensing 550 slugs per minute, in lieu of the obsolete Wyatt Earp–style rifles. To make their grand getaways, rather than a mustang, they hopped onto the running boards of a Ford V-12 with loads of power.[6]

In her letter to the editor of the *American History Journal* dated December 2004, Beverly Meyer of Walnut Creek, California, wrote of her own father's witnessing of one of Alvin Karpis's bank robberies in Nebraska in 1933. As a little girl of about five or six years old, she recalled that her father was in a meeting on the second floor of the bank building when Karpis and his bandits robbed $40,000 and took hostages as they left on their way out of town. Ms. Meyer stated, "The gang made them [hostages] ride on the running boards so the sheriff wouldn't shoot and then released them....The gang also spread tacks behind their car."[7]

In 1933, it was estimated there was a minimum of 1.3 million serious crimes known to the police.[8] According to FBI director J. Edgar Hoover's official report from 1935, one out of every eighty-four people in the United States was "subjected" to injury or death through the "workings of mass criminal activities."[9] Because many of the nation's police departments were inadequately trained in active law enforcement practices and intelligence gathering, the FBI had to assume the role it plays today.

Gangster sightings were all the rage in the 1930s in the northeast part of the country, particularly in Ohio. These murderous gangsters were feared yet revered as folk heroes or modern-day Robin Hoods. Every criminal from Ma Barker's gang to George "Machine Gun" Kelly hid out in Cleveland for a time, with the help from local law enforcement officials. John Dillinger was also known to skulk in the shadows of Ohio. In fact, Dillinger robbed his first bank on June 10, 1933, in New Carlisle (Clark County, southwestern Ohio), escaping with $10,600. Dillinger was captured in Dayton and sent to the Allen County Jail in Lima, but his gang rescued him in October in a bloody jailbreak. Allen County sheriff Jesse Sarber was shot to death during this raid.[10]

Adding to the growing list of gangsters "on the lam" in Ohio, bank robber Charles "Pretty Boy" Floyd was captured on March 8, 1930, in an Akron home. Even Floyd himself would admit that this was not his finest hour, as police found him hiding under a bed on Lodi Street in Goodyear Heights. Floyd spent three months in the Akron City Jail before being transferred to Toledo. He then made a daring escape from a train bound for the Ohio Penitentiary in Columbus, but federal agents finally caught up with him in October 1934 in a cornfield near East Liverpool. Floyd was fatally shot by Melvin Purvis and his agents. The site turned into chaos after federal agents gunned Floyd down.[11]

Less than one year after Floyd's death, Alvin Karpis successfully held up a mail truck in Warren, Ohio, and then an Erie Railroad train in Garrettsville, Ohio, with a never-before-attempted escape by airplane to Hot Springs, Arkansas. Karpis then made his way to New Orleans in the spring of 1936. But as far as great train robberies are concerned, it was Joe Roscoe from Toledo, a Karpis-Barker Gang associate, who was implicated in the colossal $1 million mail train robbery in Toledo, Ohio, in 1921.[12]

To date, this published work is one of the most comprehensive and scholarly analyses of notorious gangster Alvin "Creepy" Karpis, depicting both his personal life and criminal career. More importantly, this work discusses the enormous influence garnered by the Federal Bureau of Investigation following Karpis's train heist—a crime taking place just three miles from my own backyard. The core of this analysis closely contrasts the rise of Karpis against the formidable top G-Man, J. Edgar Hoover.

Throughout the duration of Hoover's frenzied pursuit of Karpis, Hoover found himself competing with and building on the investigative work of the United States Postal Service. The USPS claimed jurisdiction in the case and became obligated in the initial investigation. As discussed by Alcatraz historian Michael Esslinger, this last great train robbery in American history, pulled off in the historic village of Garrettsville, Ohio, boosted Hoover and his G-Men into "national prominence."[13]

Given the widespread economic depravity during the 1930s, many folks in American society had less animosity for these bank-robbing outlaws than they had for the financial institutions that foreclosed on homes and farms across the country. From the cinematic charm of the city of Cleveland to the dusty gravel back roads of rural Ohio and the icy and unforgiving waters just off the coast of Alcatraz Island, this story reads like a scene out of an

Garrettsville Opera House (library reference date November 1964). *From The Cleveland Press Collection, Michael Schwartz Library, Cleveland State University.*

old black-and-white movie. It was a statement made by Alvin Karpis that marked a watershed in the history of American crime and in the evolution of crime fighting.

THE LOCAL CONNECTION

Facing long-term imprisonment, Karpis stated with a mutter of contempt, "I made [J. Edgar] Hoover's reputation as a fearless lawman. It's a reputation he doesn't deserve.…I made that son of a bitch."[14]

Today, this quote by Karpis holds a special interest for the residents in the small town of Garrettsville, Ohio, a historic village of fewer than 2,500 people.[15] With sprawling farmhouses set high above the few winding main roads, Garrettsville is seemingly a quiet town far away from the crime that is rife in big cities such as Cleveland, New York or even Chicago. Yet today, no one would be the wiser that during the fall of 1935 this sleepy village brimming with history, Midwest charm and beautiful landscapes would unwittingly become the site of a Wild West train caper and the last successful train robbery in American history, led by the FBI's Public Enemy No. 1.

Demolition of the Garrettsville Opera House (library reference date September 8, 1964). *From The Cleveland Press Collection, Michael Schwartz Library, Cleveland State University.*

It is often said that "in a small town, nothing ever happens." Brace yourself, as everything is about to change. This is a not-so-nice story about a criminal who became an outlaw hunted by what would become the premier law enforcement organization in the world. That outlaw's legacy is introduced

Hopkins Old Water Mill on Main Street in Garrettsville, Ohio, October 1964. *From The Cleveland Press Collection, Michael Schwartz Library, Cleveland State University.*

Photograph of south side of Main Street in Garrettsville, Ohio, dated early 1920s. *James A. Garfield Historical Society.*

with a local story that left lasting national implications. During a decade that was predominately consumed by economic downfall, so lived Alvin Karpis and so lived J. Edgar Hoover. They were creatures of different environments but, perhaps, more alike than one might recognize at first glance.

Chapter 1

ENTER THE THIEF

I was ten years old…and already on my way to being
U.S. Public Enemy Number One.
—*Alvin Karpis,* The Alvin Karpis Story

As an adult, Karpis was tall and unusually slender, as distinguished by his height of five feet, nine and three-fourths inches and 130-pound frame. Karpis began his criminal career at age ten in Topeka, Kansas, where he honed a practice of robbing stores and warehouses. More than once, Karpis was described as resembling the dark-haired Boris Karloff, the "long-faced Frankenstein monster" portrayed in the iconic 1930s horror film.[16]

Alvin Francis Karpis was born Albin Francis Karpowicz on August 10, 1908, in Montreal, Quebec, Canada, to law-abiding parents and Lithuanian immigrants John and Anna Karpowicz.[17] Karpis's mother and father often vacationed in Canada, and Karpis arrived there as a newborn during one of those family excursions. Once Karpis turned two years old, his parents immigrated to Topeka, Kansas, where the family remained until 1923. Karpis had three sisters, including the oldest, Mihalin (later known as Amelia Grooms), Emily and Clara. Karpis often described his sisters as "honest and hard-working girls" and noted that his sister Emily was the sibling with whom he was closest.

In the retelling of his story, Karpis explained that it was his elementary school teacher at the Branner Elementary School who changed his name to Alvin Karpis because it was easier to pronounce. Alvin grew up in a run-down, two-story farmhouse on Second Street in Topeka. Karpis's dilapidated childhood home was located at the edge of town, where the whores, pimps and petty gamblers operated. He ran errands for these less-than-illustrious individuals with the utmost arrogance, often exclaiming that he "naturally liked the action." By the time Alvin was thirteen years old, he had left the public school system for good, completing his education to the eighth grade.

The Karpowicz home on Second Street was more than a stone's throw from its neighbors and stood smack dab up against a railroad right-of-way. Thus, it is no great mystery why Karpis had a love of trains. Throughout his adolescence, young Karpis was hopping the trains and

Mug shot of Alvin Karpis taken at State Reformatory in Hutchinson, Kansas, February 25, 1926, at about seventeen and charged for second-degree burglary. *San Bruno National Archives.*

traveling the United States. He wanted to go everywhere, and eventually, Alvin knew the railroads better than anyone. In fact, young Karpis developed all the little details that nonpaying passengers needed to know to take full advantage of the system. As fate would have it, the Garrettsville, Ohio robbery was not Alvin's first rendezvous with a train.

Karpis often described his father as someone who cracked the whip and was incredibly hardworking. John Karpowicz not only slaved away at the small family farm but also worked full time as a design painter for the Santa Fe Railroad. Karpis fondly recalled that his mother, Anna, was a "gentle, kind woman" who was easier on him than his father. Karpis nonetheless believed that his mother never really understood him growing up.[18] Given the fact that Alvin's mother spoke almost no English, this likely had some influence on their lack of mutual understanding. Sadly, it would be years later that Alvin's parents would be overheard blaming each other for their son's life of crime.

In 1923, John Karpowicz took a job as a janitor in Chicago, and Karpis moved with his parents and sisters to the "Windy City." Karpis kept up the straight life for almost two years, working as an errand boy and then a stint as a shipping clerk for a drug company. But everything changed during the spring of 1925 when Karpis was diagnosed with "some kind of heart trouble," and the local doctor told him to find less strenuous work.[19] It would be more than a decade later that a primary medical examination performed in July 1936 would reveal that Karpis was "essentially healthy" and only suffered from a heart murmur and second-degree flat feet, although Karpis himself admitted he had gonorrhea (recorded in 1935).[20]

"What a laugh that was when I think about it now," Karpis recalled in his 1971 autobiography. "I had to quit my honest job because it was too much for my health." Karpis went back to his criminal ways and returned to Topeka from Chicago where he kept up a one-man crime wave. After some time back in Kansas, Karpis hooked up with a friend who Karpis stated was "as inclined to crime" as he was. Together they ran a hamburger joint that doubled as a base for peddling illegal booze. In their spare time, they broke into warehouses and rode the rails. Karpis often described his love for the "sound and feel of trains."

On October 31, 1925, at age seventeen, Karpis was caught riding the roof of the Pan American Express into Florida, later stating that he was playing out his fantasy of "shaking down boxcars for bums." Rising above this criminal indiscretion, Karpis only received a sentence of thirty days of hard labor. This hard labor was suspended in lieu of twenty-five dollars and court costs.[21] Unfortunately, this petty crime developed a criminal record for Karpis.

THE CRIMINAL CHAOS BEGINS

In 1926, Karpis's burglary crimes got the best of him, and his noteworthy petty crime record gave the judge enough cause to sentence him with five to ten years. He was received on February 25, 1926 to the State Industrial Reformatory in Hutchinson, Kansas, where he spent time listening and learning from the guys at the very top—the burglars and bank robbers. He was assigned as a baker's helper at the reformatory. Although he was no longer a child, Karpis wasn't accustomed to a seven-day workweek. His continued belligerence resulted in Karpis thumb twiddling through his days while in solitary confinement.

One of the most influential criminals Karpis was introduced to was Lawrence "Larry" DeVol (also known as Larry O'Keefe and Leonard Barton), a safecracker, cop killer and native of Rockford, Ohio—a small village in the western part of the state. Karpis and DeVol slept in neighboring cells at Hutchinson, and Karpis described DeVol as a master at picking locks. Their

Alvin Karpis (*right*) and Larry O'Keefe (*left*), also known as Larry DeVol, were captured in 1930 in Kansas City with these guns. *From The Cleveland Press Collection, Michael Schwartz Library, Cleveland State University.*

conversations went on for nearly three years until it dawned on the young men that they should break out of that joint.[22]

It was March 9, 1929, when Karpis and Larry DeVol escaped from the Kansas Reformatory. Karpis immediately rejoined his parents in Chicago. While living with his parents, Karpis was visited by DeVol. In no time at all, Karpis turned away from his lawful pursuits and drifted to Kansas City with DeVol. For that entire year, while they were on the run, DeVol and Karpis were successful in a series of robberies pulled off in at least half a dozen states.

Over the next few years, Karpis and DeVol expanded their outfit and aligned themselves with other gang members, including Fred Barker, Arthur "Dock" Barker, Charles "Old Fitz" Fitzgerald, Harvey Bailey, Harry Sawyer, Jack Peifer, William Bryan "Byron" Bolton, John Brock, George "Burrhead" Keady, Tommy Holden, Phil Courtney and, last but not least, Harry

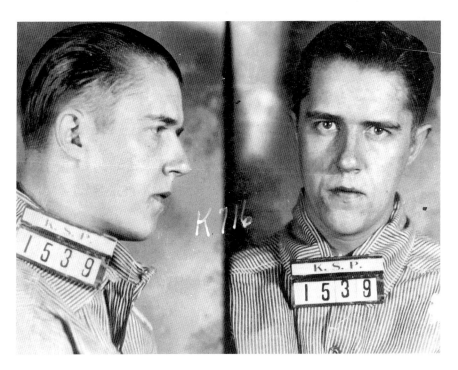

Mug shot of Alvin Kapris, taken at the Kansas State Penitentiary in Lansing, May 19, 1930. Karpis was returned to the State Reformatory in Hutchinson, Kansas, on March 25, 1930, after escaping on March 9, 1929. He was then transferred to the Kansas State Penitentiary in May 1930. *San Bruno National Archives.*

Campbell of Oklahoma. Campbell was a boyhood associate of the Barker brothers who would become a familiar face in Ohio and one of Karpis's last criminal comrades.

On March 23, 1930, the law finally caught up with them, and Karpis and DeVol were arrested on the charge of auto larceny and safe blowing. Karpis began using aliases at the time of this arrest in Kansas City, giving his name as Raymond Hadley. Karpis was not prosecuted for these crimes, but two days later, he was returned to the Reformatory at Hutchinson, Kansas, as an escapee. But DeVol was arrested on the charges of larceny and safe blowing. On April 1, 1930, DeVol posted a $1,000 bond and was released but jumped bail and remained on the run.

Due to his growing criminal record, Karpis was transferred to the Kansas State Penitentiary in Lansing on May 19, 1930. While in Kansas, Karpis connected with a new criminal collaborator who would change the trajectory of his budding criminal career.

Karpis was on track to becoming Public Enemy No. 1.

Becoming Public Enemy No. 1

Despite the era's stunted economic state, once a week about 65 percent of the American population bought a movie ticket. Motion pictures became interim distractions for folks across the country, who in one way or another faced financial fallout from the economic downturn. During the 1930s, these movies cost twenty-five cents or less. With the surge in crime, the year 1935 witnessed Warner Bros. releasing a crime film titled *G-Men* starring James Cagney. The film was a deliberate attempt by Warner Bros. to counteract the growing trend of glorifying American gangsters in the early 1930s. This moral indictment of organized crime became one of the top-grossing films of that year.

Before each movie began, a public service announcement featuring a dry voice, almost mechanical, stated in composed verse: "Dillinger could be sitting among you; he may be in your row. Turn to your right, and turn to your left. If you see him, call the Bureau of Investigation or your local police." This actually happened in theaters across the country as America entered one of its darkest, bloodiest chapters with the rise of the "Public Enemies."

When the lights came on in the movie theater, folks just chuckled. Of course, no fugitive would be brazen enough to risk his freedom by sitting in a public theater, right? Yet on July 22, 1934, Alvin Karpis and his gal, Dolores Delaney, dropped by a Cleveland, Ohio theater to take in *Manhattan Melodrama*. The film starred the "King of Hollywood," Clarke Gable, and focused on the enduring friendship between two orphans who grow up on opposite sides of the law and fall in love with the same woman.

Karpis was struck by the movie's ending, which he later stated he "didn't particularly care for," as one fellow ended up on his way to the electric chair. But Karpis explained in his autobiography that the movie didn't bother him half as much as the words echoed in the streets of Cleveland as Karpis and Delaney exited the theater. A kid selling newspapers was shouting, "Dillinger shot!" Karpis hastily grabbed one of those newspapers and quickly scanned the headline with the gory details. Ironically, Dillinger had also been to see that same movie, *Manhattan Melodrama*, on that same night at the Biograph Theater in Chicago.

As Dillinger exited the theater with two girls in tow, FBI agents shot him dead on the spot.[23] It's impossible to know what Karpis was thinking at that moment, but fear or even terror must have gripped his senses as he read about Dillinger's brutal slaying at the hands of police and federal agents. To add to the ghoulishness of this event, it was widely reported that people outside the theater were dipping their handkerchiefs and skirts into Dillinger's pool of blood as permanent mementos.

It was Albert Grooms (son of Karpis's eldest sister, Mihalin "Amelia Grooms"), of Topeka, Kansas, who at the age of seventy-two, recalled in a 1993 interview that his Uncle Alvin once told him that John Dillinger wanted to merge together the two gangs to pull off in one town "a hell of a gang and rob eight banks in one day!" That merger never materialized.

The two gangs in question were the Karpis-Barker Gang, originally led by Freddie Barker, and the Dillinger Gang, known as the Terror Gang, controlled by John Dillinger of course. Dillinger's gang comprised a crew of other American Depression-era bank robbers such as "Baby Face" Nelson, John "Red" Hamilton, Harry Pierpont, Tommy Carroll and Eddie Green, to name a few. The Dillinger Gang was said to have employed military-inspired tactics taught to the men in prison. At first, the idea of consolidating the two gangs seemed profitable, but brothers "Dock" and Freddie Barker wanted no part of that plan. Grooms explained that his Uncle Alvin was the "quiet type," and he and the Barkers didn't like Dillinger's "boastful personality and braggadocio crap."[24]

After John Dillinger was killed, Oklahoma boy Charles Arthur "Pretty Boy" Floyd became Public Enemy No. 1, and a $23,000 bounty was offered for his capture. Given his infamy, the Feds would take him any way they could, so Floyd was wanted dead or alive. Floyd was able to avoid the authorities for several months after Dillinger's death using the alias George Sanders and hiding with two women, Rose and Beulah Baird. Within several months, the grim reaper came calling. It was October 22, 1934, when Pretty Boy Floyd was fatally shot by FBI agents led by Melvin Purvis.

Special Agent Purvis had become the hotshot of the Bureau and head of the Cincinnati office. Purvis then took charge of the Chicago field office. The details surrounding Floyd's demise included a modest cornfield behind a house on Sprucevale Road and near Beaver Creek State Park in East Liverpool (eastern Ohio). After, Karpis rose through the ranks of criminals and officially secured his place in American crime history as Public Enemy No. 1.[25]

Only five outlaws were dubbed "Public Enemy No. 1" during the Depression era. By and large, this tag was considered a sort of entitlement by these ruthless lawbreakers. As a matter of fact, it was political bigwig and U.S. Attorney General Homer Cummings who assumed the standard for the Public Enemies list, not FBI director J. Edgar Hoover.

The origin of this title came about during March 1930, when Frank Loesch, the head of the Chicago Crime Commission, put together a Public Enemies list for the most notorious lawbreakers in Chicago. This designation allowed law enforcement authorities to keep gangsters under constant surveillance. Loesch put Al Capone at the top of this list. Eventually, this standard was adopted by Attorney General Cummings and inherited by Hoover. It became what we know today as the "Ten Most Wanted" list. Following the shooting deaths of "Pretty Boy" Floyd, "Baby Face" Nelson and John Dillinger by the Bureau's agents in 1934, Alvin Karpis became the last Public Enemy No. 1 of the era to remain uncaptured.[26]

As gangsters flourished in Middle America during the Depression, arguably none was more coldblooded than Alvin "Creepy" Karpis. Although little continues to be known or shared in American crime story history about this infamous criminal, Karpis was able to make his presence legendary enough to be briefly profiled in the 2009 American mob drama *Public Enemies*, starring Johnny Depp as John Dillinger.

In articles provided by the Associated Press and the *Los Angeles Herald Express* (dated May 2, 1936), it was reported that "Alvin was known to his friends by many names," including "Slim—because of his build." The newspapers also reported that Karpis was known as "'Old Creepy' because

Hoover (*center*), U.S. Attorney General Homer Cummings (*right*) and the FBI Crime School, October 1935. *Author's personal collection.*

he got on the nerves of his henchmen, [and even] Chi—because he talked so much about his favorite 'city Chicago.'"[27] It became well known that Karpis was endeared to his criminal associates and close friends by the name "Ray."

Despite his long list of nicknames and aliases, Karpis was identified by the FBI as the brains of the Karpis-Barker Gang (Hoover typically labeled the gang as such). The gang has historically been referenced as the Barker-Karpis Gang, with Freddie Barker at the helm, but Alvin Karpis remained the creative driving force behind the gang's crime spree. Karpis and his criminal associates were best known for traumatizing the Midwest during their five-year crime spree, eventually traveling back and forth to their various hideouts in northeastern Ohio. For many true crime enthusiasts, the myth of the Karpis-Barker Gang hinged on the belief that it was run by the Barker brothers' mother, "Ma" Barker. As one might expect, Karpis and Ma's son, Freddie, became like brothers.

For all its murder and mayhem, the stories surrounding Karpis's crime spree never lacked old Hollywood luster or audience appeal. Yet Karpis himself was not the larger-than-life, charismatic criminal whom Americans could cheer on like they did John Dillinger or Pretty Boy Floyd. Rather, this plain Kansas boy was a timid and quiet little man recognized for his dapper style. Karpis's cunning and dangerous demeanor was hidden behind his sinister smile and those cold blue eyes.

CHAPTER 2

THE INFAMOUS "BLOODY BARKERS"

"I'm Freddie Barker," he said. "I already know who you are.
Let's go in to supper together."
—*Alvin Karpis,* The Alvin Karpis Story

There is much to be said about "choosing your friends wisely," or rather with caution, when it came to Karpis's friendship with Freddie Barker. It is an understatement to note that the Barkers were *not* your typical nuclear family. Their days were spent plundering much of the Midwest during the 1930s.

This brood of criminal outcasts had its origins rooted in the Ozark Mountains of Missouri and Arkansas and the Cookson Hills of Oklahoma. The Barker family was infamously publicized as the core of the Karpis-Barker Gang and was composed of typical southwestern bandits armed with tommy guns. The figurehead of the gang was the Barkers' mother, Ma. She was born Arizona Donnie Clark, commonly known as Kate but affectionately called "Ma" or "Mother" by her sons and their associates.

Kate married George E. Barker in Ash Grove, Missouri, on September 14, 1892. She listed Arrie as her name on the marriage license, and somewhere along the way she adopted the name Kate. The couple and their four sons eventually moved to Tulsa, Oklahoma, although, their sons were all born in Missouri. As early as 1915, Herman Barker was arrested in Joplin, Missouri, on a charge of highway robbery. Many of the boys who associated with Kate Barker's sons later became the Barker boys' criminal associates.[28]

By 1920, Arthur "Dock" (also spelled as "Doc") Barker was sentenced to life imprisonment after murdering a night watchman. Herman committed suicide on August 29, 1927, after being seriously injured in a shootout with police in Wichita, Kansas. Frederick (Freddie) George Barker was the youngest son and quickly rose to the top as a Midwest outlaw. Reportedly, the only Barker boy to do an honest day's work was Lloyd William "Red" Barker. Sadly, in 1947, Lloyd was gunned down with a twenty-gauge shotgun fired by his deranged wife, Jean, while entering their home.

Despite the lawlessness of her sons, Ma Barker herself was not a criminal, but she did try to intervene with parole boards, wardens and governors when it came to the release of her boys from incarceration. Logically, Ma Barker could not be above some reproach, as she obviously enjoyed the spoils from the life of crime that her sons had chosen and embellished.[29]

FBI records described the Barkers as an "exceptionally poor, sharecropping family." The early religious influences of the young Barker boys "consisted of evangelistic and sporadic revivals." The father, George Barker, was described as a "shiftless" individual who did little if anything to support the family. Given the family's economic depravity, no emphasis was placed on education. Regrettably, the Barker boys were more or less illiterate.

In 1928, Kate Barker separated from her husband, George, for reasons not clearly known. As one might expect, the FBI records attribute this separation to Kate Barker's "loose moral life." Kate was reported as having been seen with many other men in the vicinity of Tulsa, Oklahoma. After the separation from her husband, Kate began living with her sons. The Barker matriarch was known to more permanently cohabitate with her youngest son, Freddie. In a real surprise, the FBI records state that Kate was "more intelligent than any of her sons" and ruled with an iron fist. These FBI records vehemently claimed that Kate Barker "cast her lot with [her sons'] lawlessness and criminal activities."[30]

On the contrary, Karpis insisted that the "most ridiculous story in the annals of crime [was] that Ma Barker was the mastermind behind the Karpis-Barker Gang." Karpis continued to refute these stories that grew up years after Ma and Freddie's deaths. Most historians, along with those criminal associates affiliated with the Karpis-Barker Gang, insisted that these stories were only manifested as a way to justify the horrible manner in which she met her death at the hands of the FBI.

Karpis was certain to emphasize that Ma was not a thief or a killer or a leader of criminals—not even a criminal herself. Karpis was adamant in his defense of Ma: "If she [Ma] had been such a menace to society, the police would surely have had her mug shot and prints on file....She was somebody we looked after and took with us when we moved from city to city, hideout to hideout…she just didn't have the brains or know-how to direct us on a robbery."[31]

THICK AS THIEVES, MY FRIEND FREDDIE BARKER

During his time at the Kansas State Penitentiary, Karpis formed a lifelong friendship with Fred "Freddie" Barker. Karpis recalled that during one of his first nights in the joint, he was on his way to dinner when a short, sandy-haired guy with "a nice grin, not more than five-feet four, and [exhibiting] a mouthful of gold teeth" stopped Karpis to introduce himself. From that introduction forward, the two hit it off. With their burgeoning friendship, Freddie arranged for Karpis to be transferred to Barker's own cell. Freddie had been in Lansing since 1926 on a five-to-ten-year burglary sentence. He was a tough and experienced criminal, and Karpis looked up to him as a leader.[32]

Despite taking to each other as they did, Karpis remained somewhat resistant to Freddie's hostile disposition. He couldn't explain Freddie's willingness to

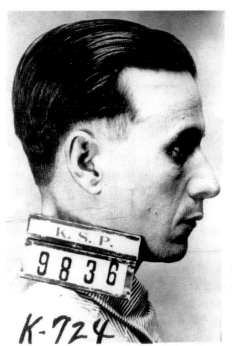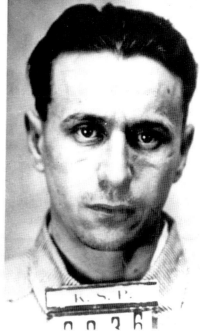

Freddie Barker, Kansas State Penitentiary, 1926. *FBI, "Barker-Karpis Gang" collection.*

settle matters with a gun. Karpis had stated at least once, "I always had to keep in the back of my mind that my great pal Freddie Barker was a natural killer." Freddie's brothers carried this same tendency. Similarly, Arthur "Dock" Barker had a trigger finger. An inch shorter than Freddie and stockier, Dock had a neat mustache, red complexion and black hair that he combed straight back. He didn't look dangerous, but he was a "lethal operator," noted Karpis.[33]

Mug shot of Arthur "Dock" Barker at Alcatraz, 1935. *San Bruno National Archives.*

Given their friendship, some accounts state that it was Freddie who originally gave Karpis the nickname "Old Creepy," as Barker reportedly remarked that Karpis's "strange and sinister smile" warranted the nickname.[34] Certainly, Karpis's menacing smile would lead one to believe this might be true. However, Karpis later told the coauthor of his second autobiography (1980), Robert Livesey, that the nickname "Creepy" originated in the 1930s, when Karpis was being pursued by the cops. During a particular car chase, the police lost Karpis's trail. As a result, a police officer abruptly uttered, "That guy is Creepy!" So, Karpis had rightfully gained a reputation of evasiveness and a keen ability to shirk the cops. It didn't take long for the media to adopt "Creepy" Karpis in the headlines.[35]

Immediately following his release from the Kansas State Penitentiary on May 31, 1931, Karpis rejoined "Ma" and his newfound friend Freddie Barker in Tulsa to carry out their crimes. It was a promising fall season in 1931 as Karpis, Freddie and some other familiar faces met up in Tulsa. In the midst of this prearranged meeting, they decided to rob the People's Bank at Mountain View in Missouri—a presumed easy take. After heisting the bank's vaults, the four men made their getaway down the main road. As they sped away, they sprinkled a stream of two-inch roofing tacks out the back of the getaway car to discourage any cops from following. Karpis's first daylight job netted darn near $7,000.[36]

Amid the criminal hoopla, the still-married Ma Barker was beginning to wane under the feelings of loneliness. During the unforgiving cold winter months of 1931, Ma took in a paramour known as Arthur V. Dunlop, alias George Anderson.[37] In Karpis's own words, "Dunlop was a pain in the ass." He was a drunk and a primitive sedentary who lived off Ma and the others. At first sight,

Dunlop appeared a slim, gray-haired guy who was reasonably neat and tidy. But as time wore on, Karpis and Freddie became more and more financially invested in keeping Dunlop around for the sake of Ma's comfort.

It was a dream of Dunlop's to live on a farm, and so he, Ma, Freddie and Karpis decided to rent a farmhouse in Thayer, Missouri. On December 18, 1931, the FBI reported that Karpis and Freddie Barker had robbed the McCallon's clothing store in West Plains. Karpis's blue 1931 De Soto automobile was spotted near the store that Thursday evening and the night of the burglary. On Saturday morning, December 19, 1931, it was reported by Carac Davidson to Sheriff C.R. "Roy" Kelly that this same De Soto automobile had driven into the Davidson garage for the repair of two flat tires. Sheriff Kelly proceeded to question Karpis and Barker. When walking toward the men, the sheriff was fired upon and killed.[38]

After the murder, the cops raided Dunlop's cottage on a report that "suspicious persons were living there."[39] The reason that the gang couldn't settle in Thayer somewhat inconspicuously was because the intrigued neighbors observed that every time the group left the home, one of them was carrying a violin case. Oddly enough, not one neighbor ever heard any music.[40]

By the time the raiding cops made it to the cottage, it had been abandoned. The police found all the items that had been stolen from the West Plains store, and Karpis and Barker were identified as the murderers of the beloved Sheriff Kelly. Dunlop, Ma, Freddie and Karpis—all of whom made it undetected from Thayer—fled to the home of Herbert Farmer. Farmer was a close friend of the Barker family and lived near Joplin, Missouri. Upon Farmer's firm suggestion, Karpis and the others hurried to St. Paul, Minnesota, for protection. It was the murder of Sheriff Kelly that first brought Ma Barker under the spotlight of law officials. Up until that time, Ma Barker was never mentioned in association with her sons' criminal activities.[41]

In contrast to the FBI reports concerning Sheriff Kelly's murder, Karpis stated that on this Saturday morning, Freddie Barker and Bill Weaver borrowed Karpis's car to drive around and check out some possible scores. When they returned, Freddie and Bill were driving Bill's "old jalopy" and not Karpis's car. Upon their panicked return to the farmhouse, Freddie and Bill warned Karpis that they better get the heck out of the area fast. Freddie and Bill had killed that sheriff. Karpis recounted that Freddie and Bill pulled into a garage in West Plains because they had a few flat tires. While waiting for the repairs, the local sheriff approached them. The boys were aware of the sheriff's tough reputation as a quick shooter. The sheriff's curiosity was piqued, and he wasted no time questioning Freddie Barker and Bill Weaver.

Sheriff Kelly didn't like the answers, so he ordered the men to stand and be frisked. As Freddie was packing and knew that Kelly would find his gun, Karpis stated that Freddie "blasted" him. It took several more shots from Weaver to bring the rugged sheriff down. "The hell of it was," Freddie said later, "that there was a bank across the street, and everybody in the damn town thought we were sticking it up. They came running down the street with their rifles and started firing."

Karpis continued retelling the story—the accurate story, he might add. As Karpis outlined, the boys got away from the station, but in their haste, Freddie Barker and Bill Weaver lost control of the vehicle and ran into a ditch; they had to walk to Bill's house to pick up his own car.[42] This explained why Karpis was immediately marked for the sheriff's murder. Karpis claimed that there were no witnesses to the shooting, and the local cops naturally linked the car to him. For years, Karpis would be hunted for the murder of Sheriff C.R. Kelly of West Plains. It was this murder that led Karpis and Freddie Barker to become fugitives of the law and notorious cop killers. In his first autobiography, Karpis admitted that he "hated" cops but claimed that he "wasn't a killer."[43]

The gang had avoided capture in the murder of Sheriff Kelly by taking refuge in St. Paul. By early 1932, Karpis claimed that Dunlop continued to do next to nothing to earn his keep. Karpis snarled at the thought of Dunlop's continued behavior—conduct that only created a zero-sum situation for the gang. Dunlop spent most of his time whining about moving or grumbling about being bullied by the young punks half his age. When he was sauced up, Dunlop would not only get loose lips with the landlord's son but also frequently abuse Ma. Because the situation had so deteriorated, "the old bastard," as Freddie called him, was found shot three times in the back with a .45. It was April 23, 1932, when Arthur W. Dunlop was found shot to death at Lake Fremstadt near Webster, Wisconsin.[44]

It wasn't Karpis or Freddie who shot him, but St. Paul bootlegger John "Jack" Peifer. Jack was the well-known and genial host of the Hollyhocks speakeasy, located on Mississippi River Boulevard. He was also a respected kingpin involved in many illegal operations around St. Paul. Freddie and Karpis often pulled jobs for Peifer, and now Peifer returned the favor by relieving them of Dunlop and making certain that the body was found far from St. Paul.[45]

ST. PAUL: A CROOK'S HAVEN

Known as a "crook's haven," St. Paul earned its reputation as the "sanctuary for criminals" in the Midwest. In truth, the city acquired this label with the help of corrupt politicians and police officials who agreed to turn a blind eye to underground activities.

Along with Jack Peifer, Freddie and Karpis became acquainted with another criminal bigwig in the underworld. He was a former bootlegger and St. Paul crime boss known as Harry "Dutch" Sawyer (born Harry Sandlovich). Sawyer was born in Lithuania, immigrated to the United States and then settled in Lincoln, Nebraska. Sawyer later moved to St. Paul, where he went into partnership with a notorious underworld boss named Dan Hogan and operated the Green Lantern Saloon located at 545½ Wabasha in St. Paul. The initial contact with Sawyer was made with Karpis and Freddie through Herbert Farmer. It was Farmer who knew that Sawyer could afford protection for the gang, which was hot at the time.

The formation of the Karpis-Barker Gang has been dated to December 31, 1931. It is on this date that Karpis and Freddie attended a New Year's Eve party at Sawyer's Green Lantern Saloon. Here the boys met some of the elite of the Midwest underworld.[46] Sawyer utilized his many police connections in St. Paul to shelter fugitives, including members of both the Karpis-Barker and Dillinger Gangs.[47] The Green Lantern would serve as the meeting place for the gang's next big score.

On December 16, 1932, the gang—including Karpis, Freddie and Dock Barker, Larry DeVol, William Weaver, Verne Miller and Jess Doyle—robbed the Third Northwestern National Bank in Minneapolis. As the members were escaping, the police arrived and a shootout ensued. Although the gang escaped unharmed, two Minneapolis police officers were killed, along with a civilian. Several days later, DeVol was captured in his apartment with $16,000 to $17,000 of the bank's money. According to testimony of DeVol's capture by Patrolman George Hammergren, featured in the *Minneapolis Star* on December 19, 1932:

> *We still didn't think we had anything but a crazy drunk and both of us took him out to the car. He was dressed in his underwear and shoes only, with an expensive fur coat over them. I made the crack about being a drugstore cowboy when we were taking him out.*
>
> *[Officer] Kast went in to call headquarters and I stayed with DeVol. I figured I would have no trouble in handling him. But just as Kast stepped*

out, DeVol dove for me in the back seat and got both hands around my throat. I grappled with him and he sank his teeth into my left wrist and hand. I kicked the door open and dragged him out onto the pavement.

We rolled there for a second and then DeVol broke away and started to run across the street. I caught up to him and hit him over the head with the butt of my gun. Kast had heard the commotion and came running out and also hit DeVol.

He didn't attempt to escape again and in a few minutes several other squads arrived and they found the bank loot and guns in the apartment. It was not until then we realized what sort of criminal we had been fighting with.

DeVol pleaded guilty to murder and was sentenced to life imprisonment. He was initially incarcerated at the Minnesota State Prison but was transferred to the St. Peter Hospital for the Criminally Insane. After the rest of the gang caught wind of DeVol's arrest, they wasted little time fleeing to Reno, Nevada.[48]

A successful escape by DeVol and fifteen other inmates on June 6, 1936, allowed DeVol to continue his crime spree for another month. Ultimately, Lawrence DeVol met his demise during a shootout with the Enid, Oklahoma police on July 8, 1936.[49] The local police departments were finding out the hard way that they needed reinforcement. Eventually, help would arrive in the form of the FBI and its seemingly noble Government Men.

Chapter 3

THE FBI

The Elite Crime Fighters

I believe in power.
—*President Theodore Roosevelt, 1908,*
writing at the hour he decided to create the FBI

Throughout its history, the Federal Bureau of Investigation has been synonymous with the name J. Edgar Hoover. Yet Hoover was not the founder. During the Civil War and its aftermath, it was the Pinkerton National Detective Agency that was utilized by presidents (Abraham Lincoln particularly) as a source of law enforcement, secret intelligence and political sway. With the recent assassinations in Europe by anarchists and the assassination of William McKinley by Leon Czolgosz (an American anarchist and a disgruntled former steel worker), one of Pinkerton's men suggested forming a government agency to surveil radicals in America. This agency would be dedicated to keeping tabs on foreign anarchists.[50]

Since McKinley's murder had made the progressive Theodore Roosevelt the new president, Roosevelt understood that his first pressing order of business would be to call for new laws that would prevent revolutionaries and dissidents from settling in the United States. Hence, at his behest, the Bureau was created on July 26, 1908, by Attorney General Charles Bonaparte, the great-nephew of Emperor Napoleon I of France and the grandson of the king of Westphalia. This official order established a new investigative division with a force of thirty-four special agents.[51]

Training at Quantico, Virginia, 1935. Special Agent George Franklin has his hand on the headlight. *Courtesy of Franklin family. Also, see Larry Wack, http://historicalgmen.squarespace.com.*

In 1909, Attorney General Wickersham formally named Attorney General Charles Bonaparte's "investigative force" as the Bureau of Investigation (BOI). The newly created Bureau had fewer than seventy employees. During the first several years of its formation, the BOI was also referred to as the Division of Investigation, but this title didn't stay for long. Between 1913 and 1933, the organization remained the Bureau of Investigation. But in 1933, the BOI was named the United States Bureau of Investigation. In the spring of 1933, newly elected President Franklin D. Roosevelt reorganized the Department of Justice due in part to the end of Prohibition, which terminated around the same time. In 1929, the Bureau of Prohibition was transferred to the Justice Department from the Treasury Department:[52]

> *In the 1935 Department of Justice appropriation, Congress officially recognized the Division as the Federal Bureau of Investigation, the FBI. The name became effective on March 22, 1935, when the President signed the appropriation bill. We've been known under this name ever since.*[53]

Since its founding in 1908, the Bureau had been plagued with an image problem. In fact, Hoover himself faced his own identity crisis, shortening his name from John Edgar Hoover to J. Edgar Hoover. His name modification was made following Hoover being mistaken for a deadbeat who didn't pay his retail credit bill. According to Special Agent Ed Tamm, Hoover was frustrated about identifying the Bureau with an easily recognizable name so that it wouldn't be mistaken for another agency. Hoover requested that his agents submit their ideas for a name with "catchy initials." It was Agent Tamm who came up with the name "Federal Bureau of Investigation."

Agent Tamm was able to convince Hoover of its marketability by explaining that its initials, FBI, also stood for the three principles that best "exemplified the character of the special agent: Fidelity, Bravery, and Integrity." Although many protested the name change because there were other bureaus of investigation, Hoover gave full credit for the new name to his boss, Attorney General Homer Cummings.[54]

The name became official on March 22, 1935.[55] According to an original FBI document, it was Bureau Inspector "Drane" Lester who endorsed the FBI as the "best and one from which we might choose our motto," which "represents the things which the Bureau and its representatives always stand: 'Fidelity—Bravery—Integrity.'"[56]

CHAPTER 4

ENTER THE JUSTICE

I think that early in his career J.E. decided that he was going to achieve something
big and I don't think he let himself be distracted from that.
—Mrs. Margaret Fennell, Hoover's niece and for many years
his next-door neighbor

Much has been written about J. Edgar Hoover's career and the controversies surrounding his long tenure as the Bureau's top G-Man. As the central character in the masterful film *J. Edgar* (2011), directed by Clint Eastwood, it is unlikely that the life lived by Hoover himself was reconcilable with the praised Leonardo DiCaprio performance.

According to the FBI, which today remains hawkish about the release of its archives, Hoover had been at the helm of this law enforcement bureau for nearly a half century. During his record-setting career, Hoover worked for eight different presidents, from Calvin Coolidge to Richard Nixon. The end of an era came on the morning of May 2, 1972. Hoover's lifeless body was found by his housekeeper at his Washington, D.C., home. To the shock and awe of Washington's elite, Hoover was found dead at the age of seventy-seven from an apparent heart attack. The coveted yet contentious seat of the top G-Man was expected to be passed to Hoover's closest friend and primary heir, Associate Director Clyde Tolson. As the country's no. 2 G-Man, Tolson never returned to work after Hoover died, retiring just two days later on May 4, 1972, the day of Hoover's funeral. He inherited Hoover's estate of $551,000 ($3.3

Hoover gazing at the Fallen Agents' plaque, August 1935. *Author's personal collection.*

million today) and immediately moved into Hoover's home. Tolson died just several years later from heart failure on April 14, 1975, at the age of seventy-four. Tolson and Hoover are buried within yards of each other at the Congressional Cemetery.[57]

As reported by the FBI, Congress ordered Hoover's body to lie in state in the United States Capitol, an "honor afforded to no other civil servant before or since that time." Soon, a new FBI building on Pennsylvania Avenue had Hoover's name permanently etched on a monolith in front of it. Yet as the obituaries were written and TV specials aired, there was an undercurrent of controversy and criticism surrounding the extraordinary power and phenomenon that was J. Edgar Hoover.[58]

John Edgar Hoover was born on January 1, 1895, as the youngest of four children to Dickerson Naylor and Annie Marie Scheitlin Hoover. John Edgar was born into a Scottish Presbyterian family of civil servants, and his roots were English and German on his father's side and Swiss on his mother's side. His father and paternal grandfather both worked for the U.S. Coast and Geodetic Survey, for which his father was the chief of the printing division. His only brother, Dickerson Jr., was fifteen years older than Edgar and became inspector general of the U.S. Steamboat Inspection Service.[59]

Edgar was raised in a modest two-story home located at 413 Seward Square, a typical yet comfortable setting within the District. From the day he was born, his mother, Annie, fondly called him Edgar, and he remained closest to his mother throughout his life.[60] As his guiding principles were formed early, Edgar became dedicated to teaching Sunday school at the Old First Presbyterian Church. Religion and debate became his interests and areas of his true mastery. Because of Edgar's problem with stuttering, he took it upon himself to research the condition and overcame this obstacle by practicing his speaking rapidly rather than in a slow and enunciated speech. Eventually putting his speech impediment behind him, Edgar learned that he could dominate a conversation. The young Hoover quickly recognized that this domination of speech allowed him to control his adversaries.[61]

In 1913, Edgar graduated from high school and immediately began night classes at George Washington University Law School. As one would expect, Edgar was highly competitive. Like his father, Edgar was interested in politics, and so he went to work for the Library of Congress in addition to completing night classes. During his studies at George Washington, Edgar also became interested in the career of Anthony Comstock. Comstock was the New York City United States postal inspector who waged prolonged campaigns against fraud and vice.[62]

The young Hoover did not disappoint, earning his Bachelor of Law degree with honors in 1916 and his Master of Law degree in 1917.[63] As a young adult and given the lifelong bond that he shared with his mother, Edgar continued to live with Annie until her death in 1938. Edgar was forty-three years old and forced to face the reality of living alone.

Enveloped by his career ambitions, Edgar had outgrown his boyhood forename. Now addressed as John Hoover or Mr. Hoover, he received his first introduction to large-scale classification (cataloguing) within the Library of Congress central reading room. This Dewey decimal system reportedly became the "model for the FBI's Central Files and General Indices."[64] The few personnel documents found in the Library's historical records department revealed that a young Hoover entered the Library's service in 1913 as a junior messenger in the Order Division at an annual salary of $360. Hoover was later promoted to clerk.[65]

It was later reported that Hoover put his cataloguing experience from the Library of Congress to good use. Hoover reorganized the Justice

Department's recordkeeping procedures and designed a cross-reference filing system that allowed the Bureau's agents to trace a fingerprint or physical description back to a specific criminal.[66]

During the summer of 1917, shortly after the United States had entered the Great War, the young twenty-two-year-old Hoover walked out of his Washington, D.C., home and embarked on his career at the Justice Department at a starting salary of $990 per year.[67] Hoover set himself apart from the other young men who entered the Justice Department. Hoover was exceptionally detailed, enthusiastic and thorough. He tackled new responsibilities and welcomed overtime work. Hoover's superiors were so impressed that they convinced the young lad to forego serving in the world war to a permanent desk job for the Justice Department.[68]

In the army of lawmen, Hoover began as a clerk in the Department of Justice and worked his way up to become the assistant director of the Bureau of Investigation. In 1919, after anarchists attempted to assassinate Attorney General A. Mitchell Palmer by bombing his home, Mitchell decided to put his eager protégé in charge of a new division dedicated to purging radicals. Without missing a beat, Hoover quickly began compiling a list of suspects. Later known as the "Palmer Raids," this widespread attack on radicals was largely part of Hoover's operation. Without search warrants, Hoover's enforcers paid no attention to whether these folks were guilty or not of insurrectionary activities. Mass arrests were made, and 556 people were deported without a second thought at the behest of Hoover.[69]

In 1924, when the Bureau's director, William Burns, became entangled in the scandalous administration of President Warren G. Harding, Director Burns was expediently fired. After six months of serving as acting director, Hoover was appointed by President Calvin Coolidge as head of the Bureau. During this time of national unrest, the Bureau was known as the most corrupt and incompetent agency in Washington.[70]

Hoover was twenty-nine years old and made it his mission to round up thousands of radical suspects across the country, especially those he felt were part of the Bolshevik faction. He had no guns or ammunition. Hoover relied solely on the gathering of uncorrupted evidence and secret intelligence.[71] There was only one prerequisite that Hoover did not meet: he had absolutely no investigative experience.

Remaining steadfast, Hoover took the job of the Bureau's directorship under the stipulations that he would tolerate no political meddling, and he wanted sole control of merit promotions. Thus, Hoover established strict rules for conduct and new lines of authority. Hoover did whatever he could to create power for his agency. At that time, agents had no clear federal jurisdiction. This would all change under Hoover's administration. Throughout the decades, Hoover professionalized the Bureau and freed it from the taint of corruption—or so they say.

It Takes One to Know One

The 1940s proved Hoover a reluctant law enforcement power when it came to rising against organized crime and the mob.[72] In particular, New York Italian American crime boss Frank Costello rose to the top of the underworld under the guidance of Charles "Lucky" Luciano. Luciano was one of the original Italian American crime bosses who climbed to notoriety during the onset of the 1930s as the father of modern organized crime. It was Luciano whose social and professional connections established the first Commission.

Luciano was instrumental in the development of the National Crime Syndicate—a name given by the press to multi-ethnic American criminal organizations. After Luciano's deportation to Italy and the subsequent exile of Luciano's successor, Vito Genovese, to Italy in 1937, Costello was at the helm of the Luciano crime family. This crime family was one of the "Five Families" that operated in New York City.[73] So, how does this backstory about the mob connect to Hoover?

Given Hoover's questionable associations, FBI agents and others seemed certain that Hoover picked up his fascination for horse race betting from Frank Costello. The facts bear out that Costello's mob rule was firmly rooted in slot machines and illegal gambling. Hoover was known to place $2 bets on horses across the country. What is usually not known about Hoover's fancy with horse racing is that a trusted FBI agent was quietly making much larger bets of $100 in the agent's own name on Hoover's behalf. More often than not, the horses chosen for Hoover were at the suggestion of Frank Costello. Of course, those horses always won.[74]

It is alleged that the top organized crime bosses and Luciano associates Frank Costello and Meyer Lansky had obtained photos of Hoover's homosexual activity with his longtime friend and FBI colleague Clyde Tolson. In an interview with Irving "Ash" Resnick, an associate of Meyer Lansky and the original owner-builder of Caesar's Palace in Las Vegas, this high-level mob courier reported that Lansky had "nailed J. Edgar Hoover."

Hoover and his aide, Clyde Tolson (*center*), being questioned by a reporter outside the Trenton, New Jersey Federal Courthouse after conducting a series of raids on white slave houses in New York, August 29, 1937. *Author's private collection.*

It was reported that Costello and Lansky utilized these photos as blackmail in the event that Hoover began a vigorous pursuit to target their illegal activities.[75] As has long been publicized, the question of Hoover's sexuality still remains in debate yet uncorroborated to a large extent.

Why does this debate about Hoover's sexuality still exist? In retired Bureau agent Larry Wack's written analysis, there's no question in his mind that the allegations of Hoover's "cross dressing" that surfaced in the early '90s "fueled the lingering fire of the rumors that existed for decades and remain today."[76]

It is interesting to note that Karpis's nephew, Albert Grooms of Kansas, claimed in a 1993 interview that his Uncle Alvin taunted Hoover for being a homosexual. Grooms disclosed that his uncle went as far as having letters sent to Hoover at the FBI headquarters. Although no one has ever located such letters, Grooms claimed that Karpis had mailed a letter to Hoover calling out the G-Man for being "as queer as a three-dollar bill." Grooms also contended that Karpis tipped off Charles "Lucky" Luciano and Meyer Lansky that J. Edgar Hoover was a "queer" during a meeting with Karpis in Toledo, Ohio. Grooms claimed that the "Giovannis"—or "spaghetti benders" (Italian American mobsters), as Grooms called them—personally showed him numerous photographs of Hoover "dressed as a woman."[77]

As a former Bureau agent, Wack considered, "Today, as was the case yesterday and the day before, there isn't any reliable historical record, photograph or witness, of either the homosexual relationship or the cross dressing allegations."[78]

Despite Wack's convincing arguments, Hoover did not get serious about moving on the mob until Attorney General Robert Kennedy insisted that he do so in 1961. Up until the 1960s, the FBI lacked any formal jurisdiction over such activities as organized crime (gambling, narcotics, loan sharking, extortion and liquor violations). Of course, Hoover stated that he willfully resisted taking jurisdiction on these crimes.

In Hoover's estimation, he claimed that these were areas of crime that most often corrupted lawmen, and he saw no reason to expose his agents or the reputation of his beloved FBI to this sort of temptation.[79] In plain truth, the reason given by many historians is that Hoover feared failure or feared to be tarred with the brush of others' failures or corruption.

This fear was likely attributed to Hoover's father, Dickerson Sr., who suffered greatly from depression and irrational fears. In Hoover's eyes, his father was described as a "pitiful figure." The young Hoover was ashamed of him. During the last years of his father's life, Hoover could not tolerate his patriarch's mental illness. Reportedly, Hoover "wasn't very nice to his father

Hoover and Clyde Tolson in May 1954 at the FBI office. *Author's personal collection.*

when he was ill." William Sullivan, a close FBI associate, believed that his boss "didn't have affection for one single solitary human being."[80]

"Hoover had a monumental ego," stated biographer Curt Gentry, who dedicated fifteen years of his life while conducting hundreds of interviews. Gentry compiled his findings into 846 pages of critical analysis focused on Hoover's contested legacy. As reported by Gentry during a 1991 interview:

> *He* [Hoover] *ordered aides not to step on his shadow and, increasingly a hypochondriac in his later years, he directed the bureau's research office to investigate medical discoveries that could prolong life. He was a man obsessed with power from his very early days....His driving force was the thirst for power—to get it and maintain it once he had it. He was the world's great voyeur....*[Hoover regarded himself as the] *moral arbiter of right and wrong.*[81]

Hoover's preoccupation with the sexual activities of his subjects has long been associated with questions about his own sexuality. Mr. Gentry drew no conclusions while documenting the director's decades-long association and close friendship with the Bureau's second-in-command, Clyde Tolson. As the lifelong protégé of J. Edgar Hoover, Tolson was the associate director of the FBI from 1930 until 1972. It has been stated that J. Edgar Hoover described Tolson as his "alter ego." As recorded in the 1988 writings of historian Athan Theoharis: "They rode to and from work together, ate lunch together, traveled together on official business, and even vacationed together." During the 1930s, J. Edgar Hoover and Clyde Tolson became known as the "Gold Dust Twins" because they were nearly inseparable. Historically, this nickname has been used to describe two individuals working closely together for a common goal.

For decades, rumors circulated that the two bachelors had a romantic relationship. Yet, "I could never find anything definitive," Gentry said. "He had very little human contact. He seemed to have no human feelings."[82]

"WE WERE THE G-MEN"

We were the vaunted G-Men once...we did our little bit.
Where now we could not qualify...to be part of it.

For now the FBI is not the group it used to be...
It is the model of success and true efficiency.

We had to learn the hard way then the things we did not know...
And as we took our chances great, we helped the Bureau grow.

We suffered heartaches and we lost the lives of several men...
But surely every one of us would do that job again.

Because today the FBI is worthy of its name...
And we are proud and happy that we helped create its fame.[83]
—Special Agent James Metcalfe

Describing Alvin Karpis as a "slit-lipped murderer [who objected] to being called a rat," Hoover readied himself to draw the net tight around gangster land.[84] Washington journalist Robert Talley contended that Hoover had "built up quite a reputation without having ever to make an arrest himself."[85] In an effort to circumvent personal danger, Hoover rallied special agents to his cause of eradicating the criminals in the underworld.

Naturally, popular imagination in American culture conflated Hoover's special agents with the famed Government Men. According to the FBI, the nickname "G-Man" is said to have originated during the arrest of gangster George "Machine Gun" Kelly on September 26, 1933. It was during Kelly's surrender to Bureau agents in Memphis, Tennessee, that the lore of the Government Men transmuted the special agents into formidable crime-fighting heroes. Unarmed, Kelly reportedly shouted, "Don't shoot, G-Men! Don't shoot, G-Men."[86]

It was because of Kelly's capture that the G-Man name was born and became the glorification of the FBI, producing an agent with an almost magical crime-fighting ability. The G-Men would have guns and cars just like the gangsters used. Additionally, the FBI National Academy was organized to train local police officers in the latest crime-fighting techniques. The Academy's first session began on July 29, 1935.[87]

The nickname and image of the typical "G-Man" would become the mascot for the athletic teams of the James A. Garfield High School in northeastern Ohio, the only mascot of its type in the entire country. The Bureau's Government Men has long been adopted as the folklore behind the school's mascot. Most old-timers from the area will attest that the mascot is a tribute

The 1934 training class of special agents (Government Men), including Milord Kirkland, Thomas McDade and others. Sitting in the first row, *far left*, is Special Agent Thomas M. McDade. *Kirkland's daughters.*

Special Agent Earl J. Connelley, undated. *Connelley Family Collection.*

to the Government Men who flooded the area after the Garrettsville train heist in November 1935, but irrefutable evidence has never been uncovered. The story of the mascot's origins remains apocryphal.

As documented by historical records, the 1934 Crime Bills did not give the FBI its authority to carry weapons. In fact, the 1934 statute "expanded" FBI authority to carry firearms (concealed or not) nationwide. As stated by former agent Wack, "[T]o believe that FBI agents carrying firearms wasn't an already existing legal practice directly contradicts the historical record. Enactment of the federal law merely made the practice uniform from state to state, much like the power of arrest was made uniform from state to state."[88]

As far as notable Government Men, it was Special Agent-in-Charge Earl J. Connelley who took over in 1934 as the head of the Bureau's special force called the "Flying Squad" and oversaw the arrest of multiple Public Enemies, including Arthur "Dock" Barker, William Bryan "Byron" Bolton, Harry Campbell and others. The "Flying Squad" consisted of skilled agents and lawmen from various states who specialized in hunting down the outlaws of the day. Earl Connelley was living in Cincinnati, Ohio, with his wife and son when he piqued the interest of Hoover and signed on as a special agent with the Bureau in 1920.[89] During a remarkable stretch in 1936, Agent Connelley was responsible for the capture of four of the top criminals who were arrested.[90] With the Karpis-Barker kidnappings, the Bureau relied wholly on the capabilities of its newly christened G-Men.

CHAPTER 5

THE BUSINESS OF KIDNAPPING

I t was March 1, 1932, when the fair-haired, twenty-month-old son of world-renowned aviator Charles Lindbergh was kidnapped. The infant was taken from his crib in an upstairs bedroom in Lindbergh's New Jersey home. In response to the crime, Congress passed legislation and President Herbert Hoover signed the Federal Kidnapping Act (also known as the Lindbergh Law), making it a federal crime to transport a kidnapping victim across state lines. This act, passed on June 23, 1932, added to the growing authority of the Bureau of Investigation. Now the responsibility for pursuing the victims and the perpetrators was given to the Federal Bureau of Investigation.[91]

KIDNAPPING OF BREWERY TYCOON WILLIAM HAMM

The Lindbergh Law wasn't going to impede the strategy of the Karpis-Barker Gang. The outlaws' first kidnapping was of the prominent, divorced, thirty-eight-year-old St. Paul tycoon William A. Hamm Jr. As the heir to the beerhouse throne, William was president of the Theodore Hamm Brewery. As some may recognize, Miller Brewing is the current parent company. Some may even recall that in 1965, Hamm's Bear mascot was the "best liked" advertisement.

William Hamm was a handsome businessman—a tall drink of water at a height of six-foot-two. Hamm Jr. had inherited his wealth and the

William Hamm, president of the St. Paul Theodore Hamm Brewery, 1933. *Minnesota State Historical Society and Library.*

brewery from his father and grandfather, Theodore Hamm, who founded the brewery in 1865. Unlike the other 1,345 American breweries that had been killed off during the Depression and Prohibition, Hamm's brewery had survived, and it had endured the underworld of the bootleggers and speakeasies. By the time of Hamm's father's death in 1932, the estate was worth about $4 million.

To the surprise of many, an informant told the Bureau that William Hamm had been making protection payments to the mob. The informant claimed, "Mr. Hamm had engaged a mob, paying them $6,000 to $8,000 a year through 'Frisco Dutch' [known as Robert Steinhardt, casino operator at Mystic Caverns] to keep another mob off his brewery during the Prohibition days…after the legalizing of beer, Hamm cut loose from the gang protection."[92] The criminals were no longer receiving their protection money, and now that selling alcohol was legal and more profitable than ever, Hamm was a moving target for his would-be kidnappers.

Just two days before the Kansas City Massacre, William Hamm was captured in broad daylight. The list of conspirators included the usual suspects: Dock and Freddie Barker, Karpis, "Byron" Bolton, Fred Goetz and Charlie "Old Fitz" Fitzgerald. In fact, the infamous Freddy Goetz (aliases of George Zeigler and "Shotgun" Zeigler) and "Byron" Bolton were both former triggermen from Al Capone's Chicago syndicate. Freddy Goetz had known for a number of years the St. Paul son and criminal John "Jack" Peifer. Considering his criminal connections, it was Peifer who originally conceived the plan to kidnap Hamm.[93]

During the sunny afternoon of June 15, 1933, Hamm was taking his usual short walk home for lunch. As he neared his house, an older, distinguished-looking fellow, Charles Fitzgerald ("Old Fitz"), approached Hamm and respectfully asked, "You are Mr. Hamm, are you not," and reached out to shake Hamm's hand. To Hamm's alarm, as he reached for Old Fitz's hand, this seemingly polished man grabbed Hamm's right elbow and tightened his grip on his right hand. A second man, Dock Barker, grabbed Hamm's left hand and arm and pushed the startled businessman to the curb.

A car pulled up, and Hamm was forced into the backseat. The car was a black Hudson sedan driven by none other than Alvin Karpis, donning a chauffeur's cap. Dock Barker slipped a white pillowcase over Hamm's head, and "Old Fitz" forced Hamm down onto the floor of the vehicle and behind the driver's seat. "I don't like to do this," Fitzgerald said, "but I'm going to have to ask you to get down on the floor because I don't want you to see where you're going. I hope you don't mind?"[94]

Karpis and his cronies traveled to the safety of the countryside, stopping about thirty miles outside St. Paul, where Freddy Goetz forced Hamm to sign four ransom notes demanding $100,000 ($1.8 million in today's dollars). Coincidentally, all the ransom notes were on Hollyhocks Speakeasy stationery. Hamm recognized the stationery immediately, as his brewery had often done business with Hollyhocks in the past.

The men then drove about four hundred miles to a house in Bensenville, Illinois. The terrified business tycoon had no idea what awaited him at the Bensenville hideout. Hamm's fears were escalated by the blindfold that firmly gripped his eye sockets. The blindfold was reinforced with cotton wool and reinforced with dark glasses. When they finally arrived at the Bensenville safe house, Hamm was detained within the confine of a miserably furnished space. The makeshift bedroom was secured with boarded windows fit for incarceration. The St. Paul heir was given a glass of milk and a hot pork sandwich.

It would be Karpis's job to guard Hamm over the next several days, and he later claimed to have become fairly friendly with Hamm during his confinement. Hamm spent his very idle time facing the bedroom wall, which quite unfashionably displayed wallpaper patterned with pink and gold flamingos on a hunter green background. At night, the terrified Hamm slept blindfolded by goggles in a bed with a headboard oddly inscribed with the word MOTHER. Interestingly, the house where Hamm was held was the permanent dwelling of Edmund C. Bartholmey, a candidate for his town's postmaster. For a cash payout of $650, Bartholmey was more than happy to provide his home as a hideout.[95]

The next morning, Hamm chose a close family friend and the brewery's vice-president of sales, William "Billy" Dunn, as the trusted intermediary for bargaining the ransom between the gang and the Hamm family. It was reported that Dunn was in cahoots with the St. Paul mob, a friend of Harry Sawyer's and a man the Karpis-Barker Gang knew it could trust. Of course, the college-educated "Shotgun" George Ziegler was to be the ransom negotiator.

Two days later, on June 17, William Dunn drove to the designated drop spot on a highway outside Pine City, Minnesota, waited for five headlight flashes and placed the $100,000 on the side of the road. On June 19, 1933, two days after the ransom was left, Karpis drove Hamm back to Minnesota and dropped him on the side of the road. Anxiously anticipating his return home, Hamm stood waiting not far from the small town of Wyoming just after dawn (about fifty miles north of St. Paul).[96]

In a quaint little cottage at Long Lake in Illinois, the gang split up the money, with Karpis, Dock and Freddie Barker, Byron Bolton, Fred Goetz and Charles Fitzgerald each receiving $7,800 for his contribution in the kidnapping. Jack Peifer took $10,000 of the ransom, and a $7,500 commission went to a money launderer in Reno, who exchanged the marked bills for clean currency.[97] Also when splitting the ransom money, a few crooked St. Paul cops who provided the inside information for the job were happy to be the recipients of some of the profits. Tom Brown, former St. Paul police chief, consulted with both the FBI and the current police chief, Tom Dahill, who had succeeded him. In turn, Brown relayed the gist of these conversations with members of the Karpis-Barker Gang.

As a St. Paul police executive, Tom Brown received $25,000 of the $100,000 ransom money. Brown received more profits from the Hamm kidnapping than any of the kidnappers. Brown was dismissed from the force but never prosecuted. Believe it or not, Brown later received his full pension. Luckily, the Karpis gang had not turned up on the FBI's radar because the kidnapping was associated with Chicago's Roger Touhy Gang, well-known bootleggers. The Touhy gang was eventually found not guilty of the crime, but by then the trail had gone cold. Karpis and Freddie Barker had disappeared into the Chicago underworld.[98]

William Hamm meeting with reporters at his home after being returned by kidnappers.
Minnesota State Historical Society and Library.

By this time, Hoover understood that advances needed to be made within the scientific techniques for investigating crimes. A Technical and Research Laboratory was established in the fall of 1932 in Washington, D.C., to enhance the current criminal investigations of the Bureau's special agents.[99] As part of an evolving crime laboratory and scientific first, the silver nitrate method was later utilized to secure evidence. According to the FBI, during the early part of 1933, scientists decided to take advantage of the fact that unseen fingerprints contain perspiration, which has a chemical compound similar to table salt. By painting the ransom notes with the silver nitrate solution, the salty perspiration reacted chemically to form silver chloride, which is white and visible to the naked eye. The Hamm Kidnapping was the first instance in which the silver nitrate method was used successfully to extract latent prints from forensic evidence.[100]

Despite the gang's methodical planning, on September 6, 1933, using the latent fingerprint identification, the Bureau of Investigation Laboratory lifted the gang's fingerprints from surfaces that couldn't be dusted for prints. Karpis, Dock Barker, Charles Fitzgerald and the other members of the gang had gotten away, but they'd left their fingerprints behind all over the ransom notes.[101]

The Bremer Kidnapping

The ransom from the gang's second kidnapping is possibly buried somewhere next to a fence post along a nineteen-mile stretch of an old highway in southeastern Minnesota. If ever found, it most likely represents part of the $200,000 ransom paid to the members of the Karpis-Barker Gang in February 1934 for the safe return of the second kidnapped victim. Edward George Bremer, the prominent thirty-four-year-old St. Paul banker with the receding hairline of dark hair, was the next victim.[102] Mr. Bremer was chairman of the American National Bank in St. Paul and the manager of the Home Owner's Loan Corporation. Bremer was also the son of Adolph Bremer, a principal owner of the Jacob Schmidt Brewing Company. Adolph was a close friend and campaign supporter of President Franklin D. Roosevelt. In fact, Roosevelt would mention this kidnapping in one of his fireside chats.[103]

The original plan for kidnapping Bremer was hatched by Karpis-Barker associate Harry Sawyer. Around 9:00 a.m. on the morning of January 17, 1934, and near the intersection of Lexington and Goodrich Avenue in St. Paul, Mr. Bremer was accosted at a stop sign. Like any other day, Bremer had just dropped off his nine-year-old girl, Hertzy, at her private school.[104] While stopped at the crossing, a man approached the front door of Bremer's Lincoln sedan, held a pistol to his side and demanded that Bremer move over. Bremer in his panic attempted to escape his vehicle through the passenger door. Almost immediately, another man opened this passenger door of Bremer's car, struck Mr. Bremer several times with a "blunt instrument." Bremer was forcefully pushed to the floor of his car. Karpis later stated that it was Dock Barker who pulled out his pistol and smacked Bremer on the head, causing some pretty severe bleeding. Like Hamm, goggles were firmly taped over Bremer's eyes.[105] The Bremer snatch lasted less than two minutes, with the kidnappers obeying the speed limit and driving matter-of-factly out into the countryside.

Over the course of several weeks during his captivity, Bremer was forced to write to his family and friends urging them to deliver the ransom money

Right: Edward George Bremer, principal owner of the Jacob Schmidt Brewing Company. *Minnesota State Historical Society and Library.*

Below: Intersection of Lexington and Goodrich Avenue in St. Paul, where Edward George Bremer was kidnapped. *Minnesota State Historical Society and Library.*

to the kidnappers. On the morning of January 17, the same morning that Bremer was abducted, Walter Magee was contacted. Magee was the contractor of St. Paul and a close Bremer family friend. As Bremer's contact, Magee received a telephone call from a man who gave his name as Charles McKee. The self-identified McKee told Walter Magee to retrieve a ransom note that was located under the side door of his office building. Once retrieving the note, Magee read:

> *We demand $200,000. Payment must be made in 5 and 10 dollar bills— no new money—no consegutive [sic] numers [sic]—large variety of issues. Place the money in two large suit box cartons big enough to hold the full amount and tie with heavy cord....You place an ad in the Minneapolis Tribune as soon as you have the money ready....Don't attempt to stall or outsmart us.* [106]

Sequential notes were sent by the gang members as a stern admonishment to Walter Magee, who in haste contacted the local police, triggering a response by the St. Paul Field Division of the Bureau.[107] On February 6, 1934, a Catholic priest in Prior Lake, Minnesota, was handed notes addressed to Magee and members of the Bremer family. They warned Magee that he'd better follow the latest instructions. Hoover later stated that the ransom for Bremer was paid near a small town about fifteen miles from St. Paul, the name of which was Zumbrota.[108]

To say the least, Bremer proved to be a less-than-cooperative captive. The gang's tensions grew as Bremer constantly groaned about his unsatisfactory living conditions. Freddie Barker became so infuriated that he almost killed Bremer several times. Shockingly, it was his brother Dock who talked Freddie off the ledge.

After incredible difficulty in securing the ransom, Bremer was released on February 7, 1934, around 8:00 p.m. on the outskirts of Rochester, Minnesota. For extra precaution, Bremer was again blindfolded with taped goggles. But despite their precautions, Karpis and his associates made one grave mistake. While en route to bring Bremer home following receipt of a portion of the $200,000 ransom money, they stopped to refuel several times. The gang didn't give a second thought to the gas cans, leaving them on the side of the road. About three weeks later, a Wisconsin farmer found the four empty gas cans and a tin funnel on his property. The Bureau sent these cans to its technical laboratory in Washington.

Subsequently, the ransom money that had been paid in both kidnappings was marked (traceable) money. On February 9, 1934, the Bureau began to distribute a list of all the serial numbers of the ransom currency to all the banks in the United States. If the ransom money was brought for exchange to any of these banks, the bank was to contact the nearest division of the Bureau. According to an interview with J. Edgar Hoover in June 1957, a fifty-year-old Chicago gambler with connections in Havana, Cuba, managed to exchange nearly $100,000 of Bremer's $200,000 ransom (tainted loot) for Cuban gold. Correspondingly, a well-known bank then converted this Cuban gold into $1,000 American bills at a discount of 0.25 percent.[109]

On the lam, the Karpis-Barker Gang hastened to Reno, Nevada. The hiatus in Reno couldn't have come at a better time. On February 9, 1934, a breakthrough in the Bremer case arrived when the fingerprint of Dock Barker turned up on one of the empty gas cans. As officially documented, it was a fingerprint lifted from one of the gasoline cans that was "identical" to the right index fingerprint of Dock Barker. By cross-referencing Bureau files, they linked Dock to his brother Freddie, who was wanted along with Alvin Karpis for the December 1931 murder of Sheriff C.R. Kelly.[110]

Karpis was implicated next as the FBI had secured the four torches with red lenses (or flashlights) utilized by the gang to signal the car with the ransom money. As with the gas cans, the flashlights were found by the side of a dirt road. These lights were equipped with red film lenses that were used as signal lights during the night. The flashlights were located when law enforcement retraced the route utilized by Walter Magee after delivering the ransom money. Bearing the emblem "Merit Product," the flashlights were traced to a specific hardware store. The store was identified as the F&W Grand Silver Store located at 67 Seventh Street in Minnesota. Through photographs, the sales clerk was quickly able to identify Karpis as the individual who purchased the lights.[111]

It didn't take long before Freddie Barker, Fred Goetz, Russell Gibson, Volney Davis and longtime Barker associate Harry Campbell were also linked to the crime. Known as Harry "Buddy" or "Limpy" Campbell, little is known about this particular Karpis-Barker associate. Growing up in the Midwest, Harry Campbell (aliases of George Wolcott and George Winfield) became acquainted with Freddie and Dock Barker, as well as Volney Davis, when they were just kids in Tulsa, Oklahoma. These bandits often ran in the same circles, attending the same grade school. It's likely that they practiced cops and robbers together out on the playground with their toy guns in anticipation of what lay ahead of them in life.

While growing up, Harry Campbell spent his time pulling off the typical Midwest crimes. It was 1932 when Campbell claimed that he first met his gal, Wynona Burdette, in Tulsa. Burdette was a part Cherokee Indian woman whose family was very poor. Campbell's intimate relationship began with Burdette after she left her bank-robbing husband. The connection with "Creepy" Karpis came for Campbell in September 1933, when Harry received a summons from his boyhood friend Freddie Barker to join the gang at the Savoy Hotel in Hammond, Indiana.[112]

CHAPTER 6

THE GOOD DOCTOR?

A fter their high-profile kidnappings, Karpis and Freddie recognized that they needed to have their fingerprints removed in order to protect their freedom. Around March 10, 1934, while in their Chicago hideout, Karpis paid $750 to an underworld doctor named Joseph Moran to surgically remove his fingerprints and alter his facial characteristics. The $250 of the $750 that Karpis paid Dr. Moran, he claimed, was for "patching up his face from the 'going over' that the Kansas City Police gave it back in 1930." Moran exclaimed that the surgery was a success, but Karpis said he was left with scars that refused to heal. Karpis described a procedure where Moran had literally scraped the meat off each fingertip with a scalpel as one would "sharpen a pencil."[113]

In the immediate aftermath of the surgery, Karpis described it as a complete failure. Later photos of Karpis would show a scar at the base of his left index finger and two scars on his ears.[114] Hoover would later agree with Karpis and reported this operation as unsuccessful.[115] In spite of whether or not the surgeries were successful, Hoover revealed that the G-Men had established 324 points of identification between old and new fingerprints. No longer could a criminal try to erase his or her identification. Skilled scientists in the Bureau's crime labs were able to reconstruct, by study of bone formations, any part of the human body.[116]

Dr. Joseph "Doc" Moran (1895–1934) was a young physician known for treating Depression-era gangsters and numerous other members of the Karpis-Barker Gang. For a time, Moran, a native of Illinois, operated a

While in Chicago during March 1934, Karpis tried to have his fingerprints removed by underworld physician Dr. Joseph Moran. *Minnesota State Historical Society and Library.*

successful private practice after graduating from Tufts Medical School in Boston. However, Moran became a severe alcoholic, and the drink was quick to dampen his medical profession. With a fledgling practice, Moran was forced to move on to performing illegal abortions to maintain his income. After one of his patients died from an abortion procedure, Moran was sentenced to prison for ten years and lost his license to practice medicine.

Moran's good bedside manner while in prison awarded him an opportunity with the warden, who made a convincing pitch for Moran's early parole in 1931. The warden also helped the young doctor regain his medical license. After his release, Moran moved to Bureau, Illinois, where he again became entangled in illegal abortions and was returned to prison—serving out another eleven months.

Resentful of his re-incarceration, Moran made connections with the gangsters of the day. These new links were facilitated by his friendship with a jewel thief named Oliver Berg, a fellow inmate Moran had treated while in the LaSalle jail. Berg helped Dr. Moran make contacts in the Chicago underworld, leading to Moran's appointment as the official physician of the Chicago Teamsters and other brotherhoods of unions and teamsters.

Moran became the go-to physician for much of the Chicago underworld, with his new practice being set up on Irving Park Boulevard. When the Karpis-Barker Gang pulled off the kidnappings, it was Moran who helped the gang launder the money through his practice in Chicago. Soon afterward, Moran disappeared.

A Toledo newspaper reported that the "mutilated body of a middle-aged man" was found strapped to a clump of bushes near a lonely road west of Toledo on September 4, 1934. The badly decomposed body was identified on July 21, 1937 as that of Dr. Joseph Moran of Chicago. Moran was well known as the fingerprint and face surgeon to the declared "defunct Dillinger and Karpis-Barker gangs." This information documented in the FBI files was obtained from federal authorities who indicated that an announcement of the identification would be finalized by J. Edgar Hoover soon. But on July 22, 1937, Hoover denied that the "mutilated body" found in Toledo was that of Dr. Moran.

One witness to Dr. Moran's anticipated demise was Edna "The Rabbit" Murray, Volney Davis's moll and an eventual informant for the Bureau. Murray contended that in the summer of 1934 and while living in Toledo, Ohio, she witnessed Fred Barker, Russell Gibson and Dr. Moran drinking at a local club. While sitting at the table together with these men, they began arguing. Dr. Moran was angry because William Weaver, a Karpis associate, would not allow Dr. Moran to operate on his fingers. Of course, Dr. Moran needed the money badly, given his material and alcoholic splurges.

True to his crude nature, Freddie Barker rebuked Dr. Moran:

> *"You have done a rotten job on all our hands and you stay drunk and do too much talking." In response, Doc Moran shouted, "Don't be bawling me out—I've got you in the palm of my hand!" Gibson then spoke up, trying to quiet Moran: "You're drunk doctor. Come on, let's go for a boat ride. You'll feel better." Gibson then turned and winked at Edna Murray. Murray knew what that wink meant—Dr. Moran was going for good.*

According to Murray and confirmed by Karpis in his first autobiography, the gang used a motorboat that belonged to someone they knew in Toledo. Poor Moran was too drunk to know that he was in any danger. Murray witnessed Dr. Moran, Freddie Barker and Russell Gibson driving away from the club in Gibson's coupe. In a few hours, Gibson and Barker returned without Dr. Moran and didn't say a word to Murray, and neither did she to them.[117] The doctor knew too much, and so he was drowned in Lake Erie.

CHAPTER 7

DIZZY WITH TWO DAMES

I never showed my women a carefree, joyful time.
When they hooked up with me, they just naturally bought trouble.
—*Alvin Karpis,* The Alvin Karpis Story

According to Karpis, there were always plenty of women in his life. He married one, Dorothy Slayman, whom Karpis described as one of "the sexiest broads in Tulsa." Dorothy was the niece of Carol Hamilton, the widow of Herman Barker. Given her past associations, Carol knew her way around the law and operated a massage parlor, also known as a "hooker joint," in Tulsa. Karpis was introduced to Carol Hamilton by Larry Devol. Carol, in turn, introduced Karpis to her young niece, Dorothy Slayman, during the spring of 1931.

Karpis explained that he fell for Dorothy the minute he laid eyes on her, and the feeling was mutual. Dorothy was a redhead, about seventeen years old and, according to Karpis, "beautifully stacked." It didn't take long for the two lovebirds to become hot and heavy, consummating their attraction only days after their first meeting. Karpis even claimed that they had chosen their own personal love song, "You Were Meant for Me." Karpis tried to take Dorothy everywhere they went, and the arrangement seemed to work most of the time. In the fall of 1931, these two tied the knot. The happy new couple rented an apartment on the north side of Chicago, where Dorothy enjoyed the quiet life for a short time.[118]

As one might expect, the honeymoon didn't last long. Karpis told Dorothy that he needed to leave Chicago and join up with Freddie down south to organize "a few scores before they ran out of money." This time away turned into four years before Karpis would see Dorothy again. It ended up that Dorothy had been abandoned in Chicago, with little consolation from Karpis's letters and the cash that he sent from time to time. Karpis would later confide in his memoirs that he felt sorry for Dorothy. Karpis couldn't risk seeing her again, especially after his presumed role in the killing of Sheriff Kelly in Missouri during December 1931. Alvin Karpis was now a fugitive; mentally, he said goodbye to his wife.[119]

Realizing that she had been abandoned, Dorothy Slayman Karpis moved to Tulsa and divorced Alvin Karpis on November 19, 1935. Dorothy was later interviewed by FBI agents, on numerous occasions. During the interviews, the agents determined that she "apparently still thinks a great deal of Karpis." At the time of the divorce, Dorothy was operating a massage parlor in Tulsa and reportedly "practicing prostitution." The FBI stated that "no help [could] be expected from her with respect to divulging information which would assist in locating Karpis or Campbell."[120]

The mourning period for Dorothy was short, and after only several weeks of being tucked away in St. Paul, Karpis met another girl who "hit [him] with a jolt," he stated. Her name was Dolores Delaney, and she was just sixteen years old. Harry Sawyer asked Karpis to deliver a package to a guy named Pat Reilly. Reilly was a middleman who handled so-called chores for Sawyer. Karpis recalled that he knocked on Reilly's door and Dolores answered. There standing in Reilly's entranceway was this beautiful brunette with big brown eyes. Karpis noted that Dolores didn't hesitate to invite him inside.

Karpis recalled that Dolores was the youngest of three sisters and the sister-in-law of criminal errand boy Pat Reilly. Born in Aberdeen, South Dakota, Dolores's sisters were Frances, Helen "Babe" Reilly (Pat's wife) and Margaret (called Margie or Jean), along with one brother named Robert (Bud). Margaret's boyfriend was also a holdup man. At the time, Margaret Delaney, later known as Crompton, was the girlfriend of Tommy Carroll. No stranger to the criminal underworld, Margaret was arrested at Little Bohemia (part of the second John Dillinger gang), imprisoned at the Alderson Federal Correctional Facility on June 11, 1934, and paroled on March 31, 1935.[121]

By all accounts, Dolores was only a kid, but Karpis was amazed by the fact that she was so anxious to get out into the world. Karpis recalled that

Dolores Delaney, common-law wife of Alvin Karpis, 1930s. *Robert Ernst, author of* Robbin' Banks and Killin' Cops *(2009).*

Dolores didn't like school, her mother or discipline. After several weeks of Karpis's visits, Dolores quit school and made a beeline for Harry Sawyer's house. Of course, Harry sent for Karpis to take care of the naïve girl. After coming to terms with the fact that Dolores would never go back to school or to her family, Karpis asked her to move in with him. In an instant, Dolores packed her bags and conceded to a life on the run, remaining with Karpis and only steps ahead of the police most of the next three years.[122]

When Dolores first went to live with Karpis, he told her that he worked for an automobile agency as a salesman and that at one time he had lived in St. Paul. Within that first month, Dolores called to mind that Karpis was gone on two or three trips—staying away three or four days at a time. After returning from his first trip away, Karpis had returned with a couple introduced to Dolores as Freddie and Paula, whom she came to know as Fred Barker and Paula Harmon. Dolores Delaney's official testimony concerning Karpis's crimes is best summarized when she stated more than once, "He'd be away for days or several weeks at a time, but didn't say where he was going." In particular, when asked about Karpis's involvement in the Bremer kidnapping, Dolores was sure to explain, "Alvin Karpis' actions did not at any time make me suspicious that he was connected with that crime." Dolores was also sure to point out that Karpis "did not want her to associate with the mob."[123]

During mid-April 1934, Karpis and Dolores, under the aliases of Mr. and Mrs. Edward L. Beaudry, rented an apartment at the Jarvis Apartment Building in Toledo, Ohio. They continued to reside there until May 18, 1934, when they both got the itch to move away from Toledo to Cleveland. Given that Dolores was in the first stages of her pregnancy, Alvin tried to spare Dolores the burden of being associated with members of his gang.[124]

The whole gang—including Karpis, Freddie and Dock Barker, Harry Campbell, Harry Sawyer and William Harrison—was enjoying its getaway in Cleveland. The boys frequented the Harvard Club for both business and pleasure. Over the next several months, Karpis tried to make Dolores's pregnancy reasonably comfortable given the circumstances. He bought her a few dogs for companionship while he was away, and the two of them spent many evenings listening to Lowell Thomas and *Amos 'n' Andy* on the radio.[125]

CHAPTER 8

CLEVELAND

First the Birth of Crime, Then the Birth of Rock-and-Roll

Often, Karpis remarked that Cleveland was a good city for criminals. For instance, Karpis boasted about the $4,000 diamond ring that he wore that had been a "gift to him by some fellows in Cleveland in appreciation of services rendered." In Karpis's estimation, gambling could never survive there without political cooperation. Gamblers spent night after night anxious to throw away their money, while Cleveland cops and politicians looked on in anticipation of their own share of the profits.[126]

Taking advantage of the fact that civic officials looked the other way, it was late spring of 1934 when Karpis was offered a job by the guys who ran the Harvard Club. The operators, Arthur and Clarence Hebebrand and James "Shimmy" Patton, became important contacts for members of the gang. Karpis explained how these guys were being harassed by a rival club in the city. The club operators impressed on Karpis that they needed a "handy gun to keep the opposition in line." His experiences at the Harvard Club helped Karpis to gain a vast knowledge of the gambling business. Likewise, Karpis managed everything from keeping an eye on the gambling tables and safe to monitoring the guys who worked for the club's opposition.

Karpis had consolidated an impressive dossier (much like Hoover's) with the names and addresses of the guys who worked the opposing gambling joints and racketeers. The Hebebrand brothers and Patton were so impressed with Karpis's thoroughness that they cut him in on 2.5 percent of the profits and set him and Dolores up in a bungalow in the nice part of Cleveland.[127]

The Untouchable City

Not only was the city of Cleveland recognized for its role in creating Superman, the Man of Steel who stood for "Truth, Justice and the American Way," but it also boasts a criminal history that engaged the mobsters in dozens of other of Ohio's large cities. In the early twentieth century, Cleveland became a mecca for the foreign-born and a city full of tough-guy immigrant kids. By the 1920s, more than half of the children in Ohio's public school system were learning English as a second language. Among the youth of the day who dominated the neighborhoods were the Italian and the Central and Eastern European Jews. In fact, Cleveland had the eighth-largest Jewish population of any city in the world. This city was full of young men who took up work as bootleggers and became involved in related crimes.

In 1925, Cleveland ranked ninth in the nation for "unnatural deaths," and by 1933, it would rank third in the nation for homicides. The Milano myth, passed down through the decades, proclaimed that the handling of murders in the city by Cleveland police was proof that the police were on the mob's payroll. The Milano brothers, Frank and Tony, were born in Cleveland. Both men became bosses of the Ohio-based crime family. The Milanos' businesses within the city of Cleveland, including a loan company and two separate importing companies in Little Italy, became a hotbed for mob activity. The members of the Mayfield Road Gang, who combined organized crime activities with the area's Jewish mob, rose to become the most powerful figures in Ohio's organized crime from the early 1900s to mid-century.[128] Consequently, Moe Dalitz became the most infamous Jewish gangster and criminal entrepreneur in the nation. In fact, Dalitz was one of the major figures to shape Las Vegas. The Milano brothers would later assume control of the Mayfield Road Gang.

In view of the growing crime, when Ray T. Miller, Cuyahoga County prosecutor, was looking over the records provided by the Cleveland police following their visits to Frank Milano's home in 1932, he stated that these records were particularly "valuable," as they could "send many of the city's prominent men to jail."[129] As was typical in Cleveland during the 1920s and '30s, bribed officials with political aspirations and achievements tried to earn their pay from the mobsters and Cleveland Syndicate.

By 1935, the city of Cleveland, with decades of boom under its belt and home to 1 million people, had crumbled under the weight of the Depression. Located at the corner of Lake Erie and the Cuyahoga River, Cleveland was once the sixth-largest city in the nation and a city of industrial powerhouses,

Cleveland postcard, 1910. *From The Cleveland Press Collection, Michael Schwartz Library, Cleveland State University.*

financial centers and Millionaires' Row. The oil, iron, steel, shipping and hauling industries that had carried Cleveland into metropolitan stardom suffered under the weight of prolonged financial instability. The metropolis now careened into a deep and lingering state of corruption, giving rise to organized crime and creating great need for strong law enforcement intervention.[130]

ELIOT NESS AND THE TROUBLE IN CLEVELAND

According to the FBI records, Eliot Ness entered law enforcement in August 1926 when he was appointed as a Prohibition agent within the Treasury Department. Like J. Edgar Hoover, Ness had handpicked his own group of agents who later became known as the "Untouchables." This descriptive term was a glorified nickname given by the media because Ness and his agents were known for their unwavering integrity. It was well known and

Eliot Ness, Cleveland public safety director, 1947. *From The Cleveland Press Collection, Michael Schwartz Library, Cleveland State University.*

widely reported that these agents had never taken a bribe, and the FBI reported that some of Ness's agents actually threw back the bribes offered by mobster Al Capone's men. Many accounts reported that legendary Prohibition agent Ness was responsible for driving the country's most notorious kingpin and his gang out of Chicago.

After the ban on alcohol was repealed for good in December 1933, gangsters earned their money through illegal gambling clubs and numbers operations. Likewise, the Bureau of Prohibition's demobilization allowed Eliot Ness to transfer his badly needed investigative skills 250 miles southeast to the city of Cleveland.[131] The Cleveland area offered two major clubs that operated openly with no regard to the illegality of their business: the sophisticated Thomas Club and the Harvard Club. In particular, the Harvard Club was a movable gambling casino located at several different sites on Harvard Avenue during its heyday. In 1933, the Harvard Club was taken over by James "Shimmy" Patton, Arthur Hebebrand and Daniel T. Gallagher. During September 1934, the casino was situated at 3111 Harvard Avenue in Newburgh Heights in the large establishment of the Walkathon Building and just outside the Cleveland city limits.[132]

The Cleveland Syndicate and the Mayfield Road Gang, which the Milano brothers had taken over, had made investments into the Harvard Club with the intent of owning the gaming operation. The Harvard Club, established in 1930, was a so-called front or "floating operation" that offered every possible game, including poker and the action-packed slot machines. This entertainment was said to have been "controlled to work in favor of the house."

The games were set in a way that they could be quickly broken down and moved out the back door. It was well known that the dealers at the Harvard Club, as well as at Thomas Club, had loaded the dice and rigged the roulette wheels as they saw fit. It was the Harvard Club, though, that was considered the most outrageous. Corruption was especially widespread there, as it was

"Ness meets the people." Eliot Ness and his wife, Betty, in a parade, just before the mayoral election of 1947. *From The Cleveland Press Collection, Michael Schwartz Library, Cleveland State University.*

the largest gambling club between New York and Chicago. The fraudulence was so vast that the press would draw its own interior sketches of the clubs and send them to law enforcement officials in anticipation of shutting down these illicit joints.[133]

As planned, the mob took control of the Harvard Club, and it became a location that everyone either visited or knew by its underworld reputation. This club became notorious for entertaining "grifters," otherwise known as conmen. These grifters were the hardboiled and tough members of Ohio society and those looking to chisel, cheat or work an angle—conmen such as Alvin Karpis and his numerous criminal companions.

According to the testimony of business owner Charles Sellers, who operated a beer parlor located at 3113 Harvard Avenue in Newburgh Heights, Karpis was a big fan of the Harvard Club. Since May 1932, Sellers had operated both a beer parlor and restaurant located directly in front of the club. During the fall of 1934, Sellers claimed that Karpis was seen in the gambling house by a number of other witnesses.[134]

In his interview with Bureau agents, Sellers reported that sometime during January 1935, he read in the *Cleveland Plain Dealer* about the escape of Alvin Karpis from Atlantic City, New Jersey. Karpis's photo was published along with the dramatic story in the paper. Upon seeing the photo, Sellers immediately recognized Karpis as a man who visited his beer parlor and was known to him by the nickname "Slim." Sellers also recalled that when Karpis arrived, he always came and departed the same way—that is, "coming from the west side of Cleveland and departing in the same direction."[135]

By December 1935, Eliot Ness was appointed by Cleveland mayor Harold Burton as the city's safety director. This position put Ness in charge of both the city's police and fire departments. The collegiate-appearing director who had once led his own federal squad of agents stated, "We find the lawbreakers [in Cleveland] growing in power. Gradually, with use of their money, they get inroads into the systems of public protection."[136]

Without delay, Ness began a suppression campaign through the police department, obviously due to the rise of gambling and vice joints such as the Harvard Club. The corruption both within the city of Cleveland and among its civic and public officials precipitated Eliot Ness becoming Cleveland's new police head. As the public safety director, Ness sought to build up the police department in Cleveland along the lines advocated by the FBI. Despite Hoover's undeclared rivalry with Ness, a letter dated May 1936 expressed Ness's exuberance at the prospect of cooperating with Hoover and the Bureau to accomplish this greater efficiency. Director Ness expressed a "keen interest" in the Cleveland Police Department's training school project. In fact, Ness inquired if it would be possible for him to have a member of the Cleveland Police Department attend the next session of the FBI's training school.[137]

Cleveland city officials at Harvard Club Raid, January 13, 1936. See Eliot Ness in center and Prosecutor Cullitan at right (with glasses). *From The Cleveland Press Collection, Michael Schwartz Library, Cleveland State University.*

As one might expect, it was the famed Ness who as a "private citizen" assisted with the raid on the Harvard Club on January 10, 1936. This incursion was the biggest single-event story in the region since the May Day Riots of 1919. In true heroic form, it became necessary for Eliot Ness, along with several police squads, to come to the aid of Cuyahoga County prosecutor Frank T. Cullitan, his staff and twenty special constables. This action by Director Ness as a "private citizen" was crucial because Sheriff John Sulzmann, of Cuyahoga County, refused to send assistance to the prosecutor's raiding party despite the fact that the raiding party had been threatened with machine guns.

For nearly six hours, the operators of the club—through verbal threats, barricades and armed with machine guns—made it impossible for Prosecutor Cullitan to gain entrance. It had been reported, although it remains unconfirmed, that while Ness and his volunteers from local law enforcement waited outside to storm the club, patrons including Alvin Karpis walked out the back door. Karpis purportedly was carrying some

Main room of the Harvard Club, emptied, January 13, 1936. *From The Cleveland Press Collection, Michael Schwartz Library, Cleveland State University.*

of the gambling equipment. Eliot Ness's raid closed the Harvard Club on January 10, 1936, but it reopened in a new location at 4209 Harvard Avenue the next month. The reopening welcomed expanded gambling facilities and a fleet of limousines for free customer pickup from downtown Cleveland. The club continued its operations despite ongoing scandals and raids until the casino was forced to permanently close its doors during April 1941.[138]

Today, an individual can walk into one of the oldest spots in Cleveland, possibly a former general store that did some bootlegging during Prohibition and then reverted to a bar after the repeal. While there, the stories one hears are as vintage as the décor—just like when Eliot Ness raided the place.

RAUCOUS AT HOTEL CLEVELAND

By May 4, 1934, Karpis's lucky streak in Cleveland was eclipsed by news that the federal grand jury at St. Paul had returned Bremer kidnapping indictments for him and the rest of the Karpis-Barker associates, including Arthur "Dock" Barker, Freddie Barker, Volney Davis, Harry Campbell, Elmer Farmer, Harold Alderton, Willie Weaver, Harry Sawyer, William J. Harrison and William Bryan "Byron" Bolton.[139]

During September 1934, the gang still possessed about $100,000 of the ransom money from the Bremer kidnapping. William Harrison and Harry Sawyer were working as "emissaries" to exchange the other portion of the ransom money for money that would not be detected by their serial numbers. On September 1, 1934, Harrison and Sawyer became guests at the El Comodoro Hotel in Miami, Florida. These accommodations would geographically position the gang to get the money cleaned through its underworld connections in Cuba. According to Karpis, they had buried the other $100,000 of the $200,000 hot cash from the Bremer kidnapping in two leather suitcases in a "hole of the garage attached to [his Cleveland] bungalow" located on West 140th Street. Only days later, these cases would have to be dug back up as the gang would abruptly leave the city.[140]

As reported in several articles in the *Cleveland News*, the tranquility enjoyed by the gang in Cleveland was again interrupted on September 5, 1934. This time, the culprits included Wynona Wolcott (Burdette), Gladys Sawyer and Paula Harmon (alias Ethel Matterson), who had a wild girls' night out at the Bronze Bar in the Hotel Cleveland. Needless to say, the girls became grossly intoxicated. News of that day reported that the three women, who were "well supplied with money and valuable diamonds," became quite "boisterous" and were arrested by policewoman Mildred Wilcox. Officer Wilcox was punched in the face by one of the women while trying to arrest them. Bureau agents learned of the women's arrest and first suspected that the women were associated with the Dillinger gang.

After the girls were accosted, a .38-caliber automatic pistol along with two slips of paper with Cleveland addresses written on them were found in their car. A five-year-old girl, later identified as Francine Faughman (Sawyer) and the foster daughter of Harry Sawyer, was found with the women. Without hesitation, Francine informed the police about the car. The police found the Packard automobile in a nearby retail store parking lot. Little information could be secured from the "heavily intoxicated" women held at the Central Police Station.[141]

Pretty little Francine told police, "They [the three women] never work and they have lots of money."[142] Essentially, the little blond girl's story led police to evidence that convinced them that Arthur "Dock" Barker had been in Cleveland during most of the summer of 1934. Police found a slip of paper in a house near the corner of West Boulevard and Lorain Avenue bearing a set of fingerprints that proved to be the same classification number as the fingerprints of Dock Barker. Moreover, the Cleveland police revealed that a seven-year-old photo of Freddie Barker was positively identified by residents living near the gang's Cleveland West 171st Street hideout.[143]

The facts of the case were turned over by the Cleveland police to the federal Department of Justice agents. Special Agent W.E. Peters questioned the three women, and then Peters set them free, stating, "There's nothing we can hold them on." It was suspected that the women were let go in order that their subsequent actions might lead federal agents to the new hideout of the Karpis-Barker Gang. Eventually, the women were released on a $5,000 bail.[144]

The reports of corruption in the city of Cleveland and specifically within the Cleveland Police Department were inflamed by the arrest of the girls. The allegations of corruption were vehemently denied by Lieutenant Bernard J. Wolf of the Cleveland police. The charges were levied by Director Hoover against the department. Hoover stated unequivocally that "crooked politicians with police connections" permitted the Karpis-Barker gangsters to escape the city of Cleveland.

Lieutenant Wolf's response to the charges was swift, and he asserted, "The refusal of the G-Men to work with the [Cleveland] police at that time [in September 1934] nearly resulted in a gun battle between police and G-Men."[145] In all likelihood, the Cleveland police believed that the Bureau was pulling rank, but mistrust among police departments was rampant across the country.

The Bureau's belief of corruption was supported by a tipoff that was made to Freddie Barker by the time he arrived at Karpis's residence around 11:00 p.m. on the evening of the girls' arrest. No media attention was given to this matter in any of the Cleveland newspapers until the following day. It was later reported by an unnamed member of the Cleveland Police Department that after the three women had been arrested, a telephone call was made from the police headquarters. That call came from someone perceived as being an officer of the Cleveland department. A call was also made to the Harvard Club to get in touch with the gang members associated with the girls. A second informant reported that as soon as the Cleveland police learned the women's identities, someone from the police department drove to one of the addresses and warned the gang to get out of town. There was no doubt in the mind of the Bureau that the Karpis-Barker Gang "was enabled" to abandon the house just five or ten minutes before the arrival of the squad cars.[146]

According to criminal turned informant John Brock, it was "Shimmy" Patton and Arthur Hebebrand, owners of the Harvard Club, who financed various criminal scores for Karpis. Naturally, whenever Karpis was in Cleveland, he contacted these two associates. The Bureau records confirm that it was indeed Patton and Hebebrand who tipped off Karpis on the contemplated raid of Freddie Barker's apartment after the arrest of the girls. It was also evident to the Bureau that the proprietors of the Harvard Club were closely connected with politicians and those in power in Cleveland.[147]

With obvious support from their Cleveland contacts, Freddie, Dock Barker and Karpis quickly disappeared from their hideouts in Cleveland. Karpis instructed Delaney to immediately go to a hotel in Toledo. From there, Delaney was told to travel to Chicago, where she soon met up with Karpis. Freddie and Ma Barker also met up with Karpis in Chicago. The gang's next "run for it" would be to Miami, Florida. Karpis and Dolores headed down to Havana, Cuba. The anticipated Cuban experience would provide Karpis with desperate refuge from the peering eyes of the special agents—or so he thought.[148]

There was little time to settle in, as on December 4, 1934, Karpis's worst fear sabotaged his tropical getaway when he spotted a G-Man lurking in Havana. Karpis and Delaney wasted no time in packing their bags and rushing from their island hideaway the next morning. By mid-December, Joe Adams, an associate and owner of the El Comodoro Hotel in Miami, Florida, had informed Karpis that a house had come up for rent. It was the perfect spot to relax, lay low and enjoy the winter season. Adams introduced Karpis and Dolores as Mr. and Mrs. Ray Green to the owner, Mrs. L. Thomas. Karpis and Dolores jumped at the opportunity to rent the cabin for the seasonal rate of $750. The unassuming house at 1121 Northeast Eighty-Fifth Street in Miami was only a five-hour driving distance from Ma and Freddie Barker on Lake Weir.[149]

CHAPTER 9

"BIG JOE"

The Alligator Leads Feds to the Barkers

For U.S. Department of Justice agents, it was the longest gun battle in the history of the agency, and one that marked the end of the gangster era.
—*Susan Smiley-Height*, Ocala Star Banner, *July 31, 2017*

With the necessary evidence located back in Cleveland, the law finally caught up with Dock Barker and his girlfriend as they were leaving their apartment near Lake Michigan. FBI agents had traced Dock through another female companion back in Cleveland with whom Dock had become infatuated. When searching Barker's Chicago apartment after his arrest on January 8, 1935, the FBI found two maps of Florida. One map depicted Ocala, Florida, which was marked, and the other map depicted the region of Lake Weir, marked with a penciled ring. These maps were shown to "Byron" Bolton, whom the FBI also located in Chicago and took into custody as a fellow Bremer kidnapper.

As an informant, Bolton advised the federal agents that these maps appeared to be the location of the Barkers' hideout. Bolton quickly became Karpis's most damaging adversary. He was originally fingered for his association with the Hamm kidnapping, and Bolton decided that providing information on the whereabouts of Freddie and Ma Barker was in his best interest.[150]

Special Agent Thomas McDade (1934–38), described by fellow agents as "the fedora-wearing 28-year-old" G-Man, confirmed that agents had secured from Bolton the details of a conversation he overheard among members of the Karpis-Barker Gang. Bolton recounted a conversation he heard among

Lake Weir cottage, Florida, 1935, location of shooting deaths of Ma and Freddie Barker. *FBI, "Barker-Karpis Gang" collection.*

several gang members in which they discussed a cottage in Florida located on a lake where there dwelled a "legendary alligator" known as Big Joe. Agent McDade stated that Bolton also witnessed within that discussion how the Barker boys spoke about "towing a pig" behind their motorized boat with an intent to shoot the crocodilian with a machine gun. Despite the alligator's historical folklore, McDade explained that within a few days of receiving this information, agents obtained the location of the fictitious alligator. With information provided by the area's postmaster, the location of Lake Weir was identified as the home of Big Joe, a popular phenomenon. McDade and the other agents accelerated into action, heading toward the address of the cottage located at 13250 27A in Ocklawaha on Lake Weir in Florida.[151]

When Byron Bolton, the former machine gun terrorist of the Al Capone gang, surrendered to federal agents in Chicago on January 9, 1935, he furnished the groundwork for the conviction of his former associates. These names would be thrown into a hat with the names of other outlaws indicted in the Bremer kidnapping case. Bolton also provided evidence for grand jury indictments in the Hamm kidnapping case. The capture of Bolton, who acted as the Karpis-Barker Gang chauffeur and guarded the hideouts, was hardly mentioned in the media. Without much fanfare, Bolton pled guilty to conspiracy in the Bremer kidnapping.[152]

With confirmation from Bolton, the "circle" on Dock Barker's map marked the spot where Ma and Freddie Barker were staying. In the wee hours of the morning of January 16, 1935, a squad of agents led by Special Agent-in-Charge Earl J. Connelley took its position, surrounding the cottage at Ocklawaha, Florida. According to FBI accounts, as soon as daybreak arrived at about 7:00 a.m., Special Agent Connelley called out to the Barkers that the house was surrounded. Agent Connelley cautioned the Barkers that they would not be harmed if they "left the house one at a time." Connelley also warned the Barkers that if they did not leave immediately, the agents would have to gas the house and drive them out.

The agents waited about fifteen minutes to no avail. After twenty minutes, the agents shot a tear gas shell into the house, and immediately Ma Barker was heard screaming. It went silent for a few minutes. During this interval, agents surrounding the house called out to the Barkers to surrender, again without response. Agent Connelley once more commanded them to come out of the house. Agents reported that Kate Barker called out in "a rather distinct tone of voice, 'All right—go ahead.'" To the agents, it appeared that the Barkers were going to come out and surrender.

Just moments later, someone on the second floor in the front bedroom fired 25 to 30 machine gun bullets at Agent Connelley, who was standing about thirty yards from the house. This barrage of bullets made it obvious to the agents that Freddie Barker fired a rifle from the front lower floor of the house and through the front door, although no details were given as to why. As soon as this firing started from Barker, Agent White, who was covering Connelley, shot a .351 rifle into the house. Knocked from his footing, Connelley fell back and accidentally fired off his rifle. In response, gunfire from the house was spread over the yard and volleyed toward Agent White. The other agents began firing into the house, and the brutal exchange continued for two hours. It was estimated that the agents fired about 500 rounds into the house and that Fred and Ma shot off about 250 rounds.[153]

After firing from inside the house had ceased and reasonable time had passed, Willie Woodbury, the young black caretaker of the property, curiously agreed to go into the house. He was anxious to see whether the Barkers were still alive. According to Special Agent Thomas McDade, it was the "kidding around" and a joking proposition by one of the agents that prodded the young man into the famous death scene. The joke started out with an agent offering Willie a few dollars, and it quickly climbed to ten dollars if he'd go into the cottage to see if the Barkers were dead or alive.

Willy wasted no time:

> *"For ten dollars, I'd do it. But you gotta make it look like you is* [sic] *making me do it." With the many agent voices raised in high spirit, Willie confidently strolled up to the house and entered through the screen door. After several minutes, Willy stuck his head out from the upstairs window, and in his "slow Southern speech he drawled, 'They all daid* [dead].'"[154]

The agents received the go-ahead from Willie. In the upstairs bedroom, agents found Fred Barker surrounded by blood and lying in the middle of the bedroom. Freddie was facedown with a .45 automatic pistol underneath him and a machine gun just beyond his left hand. Ma was found in the northeast corner of this same room.[155]

In the written account of Agent McDade, Kate Barker was found lying on her side behind the door, and her arm was "cradling a Thompson sub-machine gun with a hundred-shot drum which she had been firing. A .45 caliber pistol, damaged by a bullet which had hit it, lay near her wounded hand."[156]

The bodies of the Barkers remained untouched until arrangements were made with the coroner. Once they scavenged the bodies, $14,312 was recovered. Four $1,000 bills were recovered from a money belt worn by Fred Barker, and ten $1,000 bills were recovered from the pocketbook of Kate Barker. According to the FBI, none of this money could be identified as part of the Bremer kidnapping ransom amount.[157]

As described by J. Edgar Hoover, the special agents also found an "interesting exhibit" in the Barker cottage at Lake Weir. It was a letter from Dock Barker in which it was written: "I took care of that business for you boys…I am like Standard Oil—always at your service. Ha ha!" That "business" was the matter of murder! William J. Harrison, who had moved within the orbit of the Capone Syndicate and the Karpis-Barker Gang, was executed. It was well known that Harrison's reliability had come under scrutiny by the Barker mob. Thus, from his Florida hideout, Freddie Barker ordered the execution of Harrison, and Dock Barker had seen to it. Hoover said that late one night Dock Barker took Harrison out to an abandoned barn near Ontarioville, Illinois, and shot him to death. After fatally shooting Harrison, Dock saturated him and the surrounding area with gasoline and torched the whole place.[158]

Throughout the decades, the Barkers' fatal shooting by Bureau agents remained controversial. By the turn of the second millennium, it was veteran Bureau agent Larry Wack who pointed out that Special Agent Thomas McDade, present during the entire Barker shootout, was the only person on site with a camera. After the shooting stopped and agents entered the home, McDade's crime scene photos clearly revealed Ma Barker with a Thompson machine gun. As explained by Wack:

While some will contend that this was a staged cover up by the Bureau, her shooting at agents is corroborated by others present. Regardless of

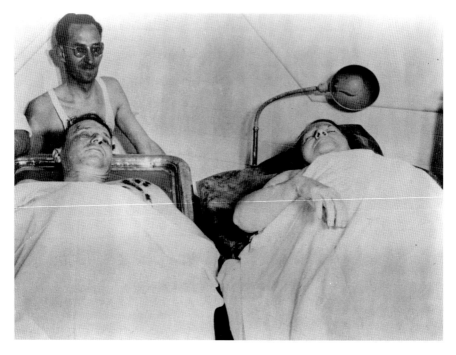

Freddie and Ma Barker displayed at the coroners. *FBI, "Barker-Karpis Gang" collection.*

being a woman or not, or having no prior arrest record, the fact of life is that if you're going to pick up a weapon, point it, and shoot it at law enforcement officers, you probably should prepare yourself to be taken home in a body bag![159]

The official FBI website states that the "agents responded with volleys of their own; more gunfire erupted from the house. Over the next hour, intermittent shots came from the home, and agents returned fire. By 10:30 a.m., all firing had stopped. Both Ma and Fred, it was soon learned, were dead."[160]

That same day of January 16, 1935, after she heard on the radio about the fatal shooting of Ma and Freddie Barker at Lake Ocklawaha, Dolores's phone rang. It was a usually quiet afternoon around 3:00 p.m., and the quick but stern voice on the other end asked for Ray Green. Dolores told the gentleman that Ray was not in but that she was his wife. The mysterious man on the other end of that phone pleaded with Dolores to "leave the house immediately." Later, Dolores found out that this warning call came from "Duke" Randall, a longtime Karpis-Barker associate.[161]

CHAPTER 10

THE ONES WHO GOT AWAY

On January 19, 1935, the Associated Press reported that Alvin Karpis's mother was appealing to her only son to surrender to the law. "Give yourself up, son—don't wait for them to shoot you down," she begged.[162]

Alvin "Creepy" Karpis, the recently dubbed "Public Enemy No. 1," had other things on his mind. His primary concern was getting the heck out of Florida and fast. Just after midnight on Saturday, January 19, Karpis and his criminal comrade Harry Campbell arrived exhausted but safe by car and checked into the Dan-Mor Hotel on Kentucky Avenue. The hotel was just three blocks from the boardwalk in Atlantic City. The boys finally had a moment to try to grasp the reality of the deaths of Ma and Freddie. The girls, Delaney and Burdette, had arrived by train into the city the previous day. Exhausted herself, Delaney was due to give birth at any time. On that Saturday afternoon, Karpis, Campbell and their girls spent the better part of the day scaling through retail stores and picking up winter clothes and other necessities. While out, Karpis, in his usual state of heightened paranoia, noticed a man and woman whom he had seen earlier that morning and suspected that they were being followed.

Meanwhile, Agent Connelley, who was tying up loose ends following the shooting deaths of Ma and Freddie, had already ordered a description of Karpis and Campbell's car broadcast to police departments on the Eastern Seaboard. Early Sunday morning, January 20, an officer near the Atlantic City Boardwalk found the Buick and matching plate number mentioned in Connelley's broadcast. The criminals' car was sitting at the Coast Garage on

Kentucky Avenue. The officer notified his captain, and three detectives were dispatched to the garage. The attendant at the garage told the detectives that the car belonged to someone staying at the Dan-Mor Hotel.[163]

It was no time at all before the police caught up with Karpis, Campbell and their girls at the hotel.[164] Narrowly escaping after a gunfight with police, Karpis and Campbell were again on the run. Karpis claimed that he had to leave his pregnant teenage girlfriend behind. While trying to escape the hotel during the shootout, Delaney was accidentally struck in the leg and unable to flee the scene. Dolores and Wynona were taken into temporary custody by federal agents and transported to Philadelphia, Pennsylvania. Both Dolores and Wynona entered a plea of guilty to charges of harboring a fugitive in a Miami Federal Court. As a mother-to-be, Dolores was sentenced to a five-year term at the United States Detention Farm in Milan, Michigan.[165]

After her capture, Dolores reluctantly reported to Bureau agents that she had heard that Karpis and Campbell had fled to Cleveland, then on to Toledo and then somewhere out west to lay low. When again questioned by Bureau agents about the places that Karpis and Campbell might go, Dolores stated that there were only two places that she knew of. One place was the Harvard Club, and the other was a tavern located about one block off Euclid Avenue and just outside downtown Cleveland. Obviously, Karpis was keen enough to know that if Dolores was captured it would be wise if she believed these were the places where he'd return. Following Delaney's testimony, Agent Connelley, with little enthusiasm, began to spearhead the investigation already underway in Cleveland to locate Karpis.[166]

By the time their seven-pound baby boy, named Raymond Alvin, was born on February 1, 1935, Karpis would be shacked up in a whorehouse in Toledo, Ohio. Karpis was taking solace with a middle-aged madam named Edith Barry. It was Barry who brought the papers into Karpis with the announcement of his son's birth. Karpis described Barry as "a good broad," but he didn't love her. Karpis claimed that he only had thoughts for Dolores. He explained that Barry "just liked going to bed with him." Karpis's intuitions were solid, and Edith Barry had the best connections in Toledo. Karpis knew that he'd never see Dolores again, and he never crossed paths with her for the rest of their lives.[167]

Both Dolores and Wynona received five-year sentences and were incarcerated together at the women's federal detention farm in Milan, Michigan. Now, Hoover and his G-Men were in the race of their careers to locate Karpis and Campbell through any methods necessary. In a memorandum written to Director Hoover, Agent Muzzey stated that he

Dolores Delaney's mug shot, dated January 10, 1936. *Maryland National Archives.*

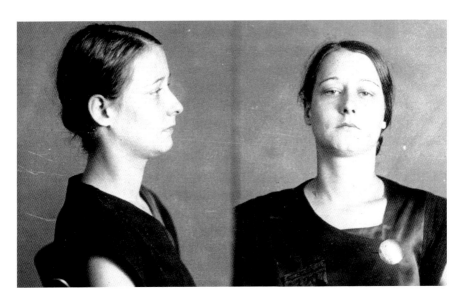

Wynona Burdette's mug shot, dated January 10, 1936. *Maryland National Archives.*

overheard a conversation between Wynona Burdette and her sister, Mrs. R.D. Wilson. In an effort to gain information about the whereabouts of Karpis and Campbell, Muzzey strategically hid in a corner behind a filing cabinet in the visiting room. During the conversation between Wynona and her sister, Wilson indicated that she could not sleep at night because she dreaded the thought of Harry Campbell paying her a visit. Why?

Wilson exclaimed that she "was scared to death that Karpis might be with [Campbell]." Wynona also admitted that she was "scared to death of Karpis." In fact, Wynona shared with her sister that "Karpis was mean" and that during the time of their stay in Florida, Harry would not let her come into contact with him.

Wynona seemed bewildered about Dolores's relationship with Karpis. She concluded that Dolores "certainly picked a lemon when she picked Karpis, that he was ugly, had big feet, long legs and a long face and was as mean as the dickens." When Wynona asked her sister to keep Harry's watch chain and a certain set of pajamas of Harry's for her, it was apparent to the eavesdropping agent that Wynona was still madly in love with Campbell. Fortunately or not for Wynona, Campbell was still on the loose and up to no good.[168]

CHAPTER 11

GANGSTERS REVISIT
NORTHEASTERN OHIO

Nobody stopped a doctor's car.…He [Hunsicker] *told us that if he didn't turn up for a few hours, no one would miss him.*
—*Alvin Karpis,* The Alvin Karpis Story

The attention of the man-hunters was now focused back in northeastern Ohio. At around ten o'clock on Monday evening, a man, shaken to his core, telephoned the Wadsworth Police Department to inform it that he was kidnapped. The unidentified man, a Philadelphia psychiatrist, claimed that he had been kidnapped near Allentown, Pennsylvania. One of the two unknown captors was thought to be Uncle Sam's newest Public Enemy No. 1. The victim, Dr. Horace Hunsicker, who was the son of a Pennsylvania state senator and an associate house physician at the state hospital for the insane in Allentown, told a thrilling story.

On Sunday, January 20, 1935, Dr. Hunsicker was driving to the hospital around midnight when a car sped up beside his. A man leaned out of the car with a machine gun, ordering him to stop. Hunsicker saw two men in the car. One of the men, later identified by Hunsicker as Karpis, got out and entered his car and then ordered him to follow the other car, driven by Harry Campbell. After a few miles, the captors' car was abandoned, and all three men got into Hunsicker's car. The men took the 450-mile ride to the Guilford Grange Hall (located near the city of Medina), where Hunsicker was abandoned. Hunsicker told his story first to Wadsworth police chief Tommy Lucas and Officer T.W. Welday, who then called the sheriff. Hunsicker was later taken to the Park Hotel, where he retold his story to federal agents and reporters. Dr. Hunsicker's abandoned car was found in Monroe, Michigan, that Tuesday morning.

An examination of the Guilford Grange Hall substantiated Dr. Hunsicker's story. The kidnappers had busted out a window light in the back door, enabling the kidnappers to reach in and release the bolt that held the door tight. Hunsicker was taken into the main meeting hall and left in a small room that was located at the back of the hall beside the stage. He was bound with his own belt, part of a suit of pajamas and some electric wiring torn from the walls of the hall. After abandoning him, the gangsters continued their flight in the doctor's car. According to Hunsicker, it took nearly an hour for him to free himself. From the hall, he fled to the home of Sam Derhammer, the first house east of the hall, but couldn't obtain a phone there. Hunsicker then walked to the home of Jerome Critz, and from there he telephoned the Wadsworth police.[169]

In Karpis's account of the kidnapping:

> We plotted a route across the Delaware River into Pennsylvania and across to the friendly cities of Ohio. We had to switch cars. On the highway near Allentown, we came across a 1934 Plymouth with doctor's emblems on the rear bumper. It might have been custom-made for us. He [Hunsicker] was the ideal victim for us, and we treated him with absolute politeness. He, in turn, didn't seem especially nervous, and the bunch of us got along like old buddies....[Although, after Lowell Thomas came on the radio and announced that the entire Eastern Seaboard was] barricaded against two desperate gunmen who had shot their way out of Atlantic City, all of a sudden our friendly doctor was anxious to leave us.[170]

Karpis recalled that after leaving the terrified doctor tied up with a gag around his mouth and a fifty-dollar bill stuffed into his breast pocket (to pay his way home back to Pennsylvania), he and Harry took off for Toledo in the doctor's car.

As far as the Hunsicker kidnapping, which brought national attention to Wadsworth, it was Chief Tommy Lucas of the Wadsworth State Police Bureau who took up the story. Lucas stated, "Doctor Hunsicker told me both men were well clothed, and both were armed with submachine guns, which they kept pointed at his back while he drove. They did not stop for food."

Chief Lucas, who became Wadsworth's Mayor Lucas, was a familiar sight on his motorcycle in Wadsworth, which became a city in 1931. For twelve

Dr. Horace Hunsicker viewing photos of Karpis and Campbell. *Author's private collection.*

Wadsworth police chief Tommy Lucas (*left*) pictured with Dr. Horace Hunsicker (*right*) following Hunsicker's kidnapping, January 1935. *Roger Havens, Wadsworth Schools and Wadsworth Area Historical Society (Northeast Ohio).*

Chief Tommy Lucas on his motorcycle, 1932. *Roger Havens, Wadsworth Schools and Wadsworth Area Historical Society.*

years, "Tommy," as he was called by everyone, served as the village health officer and for seventeen years as a truant officer. Two of the high points of Tommy's service included the 1918 influenza epidemic, in which he cared for many of the patients himself, and the dramatic attempt to capture Karpis. It was Lucas who put the word on the state police radio, and a trap was spread for the two desperadoes.[171]

More than eighty years later, Sheriff Tommy Lucas's great-grandson Duane Blubaugh shared with me his own recollections of this story of his great-grandfather. Blubaugh noted that after his great-grandfather's radio APB, the search for Karpis extended into Sheriff Lucas's jurisdiction. Blubaugh stated:

> *I did hear that Harry Campbell, Alvin Karpis, and captured Dr. Hunsicker got along pretty well. They even tied him up loose at the Guilford Grange so that he could easily escape. I don't know much about Dr. Hunsicker's captivity. In fact, I only remember a couple of times that I saw my great-grandfather. I was born in 1955, and he passed in 1964.[172]*

CHAPTER 12

THE NEXT-TO-LAST SCORE

Some people steal to stay alive, and some steal to feel alive. Simple as that.
—V.E. Schwab, American fantasy author best known for her 2013 novel Vicious

After fleeing Wadsworth, Karpis and Campbell again tucked themselves away at Edith Barry's prostitution house in Toledo. It was the last days of January 1935, and the gang shuffled between Barry's place and various other rooming houses in Toledo. Eventually, Dolores gave her testimony to the FBI, telling the Bureau only of some of Karpis's hangouts in Toledo and Cleveland and of his obsession with fishing.[173]

Karpis claimed that he was paying top dollar for protection and utilizing his old connections to find new criminal associates who had not yet shown up on the FBI radar.[174] By April 22, 1935, Alvin Karpis, Dock Barker, Charles Fitzgerald, Edmund Bartholmey, Byron Bolton, Jack Peifer and Elmer Farmer were indicted for the kidnapping of brewer William Hamm. The U.S. Department of Justice offered a $5,000 reward for the capture of Barker and Karpis.[175]

Just two days after the Hamm indictment, Karpis anticipated a new score hatched by criminal newcomer Freddie Hunter. Karpis and Harry Campbell planned to take the payroll from the Youngstown Sheet and Tube plant in Warren, Ohio. As a new arrival to the nearly extinct Karpis-Barker Gang, Fred John Hunter, an ex-con in his mid-thirties, was a former gas welder who turned gambler, card dealer, devotee of cockfighting and remained an ex-convict from Warren.[176] On October 13, 1899, Hunter was born and also raised in Warren, another Ohio city situated in the northeast. For American history enthusiasts, Warren (Trumbull County) was the city of astronaut Neil Armstrong's first airplane ride back in 1936, when Armstrong was just shy of his sixth birthday.

Warren became an unhappy place for Freddie Hunter. Sadly, Freddie's mother died at a young age in 1910, and his emotionally disconnected father, George, worked as a blacksmith and boilermaker to provide for his five children. Hunter's only sister was adopted after the death of his mother, and Hunter's two older brothers were taken to a farm in Garrettsville and provided for by a "Mrs. Alford" in return for help on her farm. The boys received an education and living accommodations. It was reported that the two brothers only stayed a short time and then ran away to join the navy. Years after his mother's passing, Hunter's father turned bitter toward his children.[177]

Hunter's physical appearance represented a man poorly nourished. He had dark chestnut hair, gray-blue eyes and an occasional dark mustache. Never married, Hunter stammered over long words when nervous or excited and seemed socially awkward and emotionally unsettled. Hunter was first arrested by the Toledo Police Department on June 3, 1920, for carrying a concealed weapon. About two years later, on October 28, 1922, Hunter was again arrested by the Akron Police Department as a fugitive from justice. Hunter kept up his criminal ways and was convicted of larceny and possession of dynamite.

On April 17, 1933, Hunter was received at the Ohio State Penitentiary in Columbus to serve an "indeterminate sentence" of three to twenty-seven years.[178] A lifelong resident of the northeastern Ohio area, it was Hunter who brought up the idea of knocking off a mail truck in Warren.[179] Hunter couldn't participate in this job, as he was too well known in the area. Excited yet anxious, this was the first job that Karpis had pulled off in a while and since the death of his dearest friend and former associate Freddie Barker.

On April 27, 1935, the *Cleveland Press* reported that Burl Villers, a United States mail truck driver, was "relieved" of $124,000 in cash and bonds ($72,000 in currency and more than $50,000 in government bonds) by three men. This robbery was conducted as Villers drove away from the Warren railroad station to the post office on the afternoon of Wednesday, April 24, 1935. The job involved just Karpis, Harry Campbell and newcomer Joe Rich. As the availability of credentialed conmen was sparse, Freddie Hunter threw Joe Rich's name into the hat for the Warren

Fred Hunter's Alcatraz mug shot, 1937. *San Bruno National Archives.*

job. Despite Rich's paltry qualities, Karpis regarded him as a "pretty good guy" when he met him. Karpis recalled that Rich was "a narcotics addict" who "lived with the madam of a whorehouse in Canton, Ohio. He had plenty of nerve, he promised to keep his narcotics habit under control... and he was satisfied to leave all the planning and directing to us." Karpis made that clear.[180]

They arrived at the Warren depot that afternoon. Harry Campbell and Joe Rich got out of the car and ambled over to the station's platform ahead of the train's arrival, where the mail truck was waiting. They were concealing their pistols under their coats, and Harry quickly became uneasy due to the peering eyes of the station's employees.

Harry became so spooked that he and Joe rushed back to the car, where Karpis was behind the wheel. Harry and Joe jumped back into the car, and Karpis drove around for a few blocks until Harry calmed down. Karpis continued to angle through the streets until he located the mail truck. Once he spotted it, Karpis pulled his car in front of it, blocking the driver's path.

Joe and Harry jumped out, pulled their pistols and quickly apprehended the driver, who had just dropped a pistol from his quivering hand out the truck window. They drove several blocks to a nearby garage while sirens were wailing far behind them.

Karpis, Harry and Joe made it to an abandoned barn, where they had arranged to meet Freddie Hunter. They immediately ripped open the sacks on the barn floor and were dazzled by the sight of twelve thousand $1 bills, with the remaining large bills adding up to $72,000. They split the $60,000 into three shares, Hunter got $5,000 for suggesting the job, and the rest went toward expenses. Poor Joe Rich had never seen so much money. Karpis said that Joe was so excited that he decided he needed a morphine fix right then and there in the barn. Without any water to boil his morphine, he improvised by draining the water out of the car radiator. He heated the water and morphine with a homemade fire and poured the solution into a syringe. Without a moment's hesitation, Joe stuck the hypodermic needle into his arm. Karpis recalled that ten minutes after his fix, Joe was exclaiming that they should heist the Federal Reserve Bank in Cleveland.[181]

Only several hours had passed when two well-known Akron criminals—known as George Sargent and Tony Labrizetti (alias Tony Campo)—were wrongfully identified as the robbers by Burl Villers, the mail truck driver. Because of Villers's testimony, the two men were charged, convicted and sentenced to twenty-five years in a federal penitentiary. They were granted a new trial but were convicted at the second trial as well. Later investigation revealed that the two were innocent of the crime and that Karpis and Campbell were the guilty parties.[182]

It was the United States Postal Inspection Service that became involved in the original investigation. The USPIS was responsible for the recovery of the transported U.S. mail.[183] The search focused on Akron because a mail sack containing $52,000 in bonds was found floating in the Portage Lakes Reservoir near the city. These registered securities brought four postal inspectors to Akron to assist with the search. The post office inspectors announced a reward of $2,000 for information leading to the capture of this "holdup trio."[184] It was not until years later that law enforcement officials realized that the two Akron men were falsely convicted.[185]

After the mail truck robbery, Karpis and Campbell returned to Tulsa, Oklahoma, where they visited an old pal from the Central Park Gang named George "Burrhead" Keady. Since Karpis was trying to revive the Karpis-Barker Gang by recruiting new members, Keady put Karpis in touch with a local hoodlum named John Brock. Brock was a young man with an extensive criminal record who served time in the Oklahoma State Penitentiary with Dock Barker. Eventually, Brock made his way to Toledo, where he connected with Karpis at Edith Barry's place located at 524 Southard Avenue. With some funds from their Warren robbery, they planned their very last criminal venture.[186]

CHAPTER 13

THE LAST GREAT
TRAIN ROBBERY

I thought of the bandits of the old West, the James Brothers,
the Dalton Boys, and all the rest of them. They knocked over trains,
and I was going to pull the same stunt.
—*Alvin Karpis*, The Alvin Karpis Story

Believe it or not, Karpis claimed that he wasn't "necessarily" needing the cash by the fall of 1935. What drove Karpis into action was his acknowledged "desire to be busy." Karpis proclaimed, "I was aching for an exciting heist."

The era's last Public Enemy had been planning the robbery of a mail train for weeks, and Karpis had his eye on the mail train that carried payrolls from the Federal Reserve Bank in Cleveland to small Ohio towns. Karpis took into his planned train caper five experienced stick-up guys: Freddie Hunter, Harry Campbell, John Brock, Benson "Soup" Groves (alias Ben Grayson) and the seasoned Sam Coker. As a native of West Virginia, Benson Groves was the newcomer, recommended by criminal companion Joe Roscoe. As an older and experienced robber in his fifties, Groves had recently been released from prison after knocking over a post office in New Jersey.[187]

Although the guys were all sold on the job, Karpis recalled that it was Benson Groves who dared to question Karpis with an intimation of skepticism: "Who the hell robs a train in this day and age?" Karpis's rebuttal was just one of his mischievous and half-cocked attempts at a smile. Karpis was confident in his strategy, and his history of criminal successes convinced him of a victorious and profitable result:

Garrettsville, Ohio train depot, November 1935. *Original photo courtesy of James A. Garfield Historical Society.*

My profession was robbing banks, knocking off payrolls, and kidnapping rich men. I was good at it. Maybe the best in North America for five years, from 1931 to 1936....I might have made it to any high position that demanded brains and style and a cool, hard way of handling yourself. Certainly I could have held the highest job there was in any line of police detection work. I outthought, outwitted, and just plain defeated enough cops and G-Men in my time to recognize that I was more knowledgeable about crime than any of them, including the number-one guy, J. Edgar Hoover....I became a robber, a heister, and a kidnapper. And I was a pro![188]

Expecting $300,000 in cash, Karpis knew that the Erie train coming from Cleveland would be carrying the weekly payrolls from the Federal Reserve Bank to the giant mills of Youngstown and Warren. This transport of cash would include a stop at the quaint Garrettsville, Ohio train depot. Karpis set the date of November 7, 1935, for what would become one of the greatest heists in American history. He recognized that the Garrettsville depot had the advantage of proximity to the inconspicuous Port Clinton Airport but a disadvantage of its nearness to a busy college town named Hiram.

As an astute criminal, Karpis cased the trains and ran the roads between Garrettsville and Port Clinton numerous times—he memorized every bump along the way. The plan concluded with an escape from the Garrettsville depot by car and a final departure from Port Clinton by airplane—a stunt never attempted before Karpis had carried it out.[189]

In late May 1935, Freddie Hunter left for Hot Springs, Arkansas, to seek treatment for a venereal disease—gonorrhea, in fact. While in Hot Springs, Hunter searched for a place to take refuge somewhere for him and Karpis to lay low while the FBI hunt intensified. Hunter returned to Warren a few weeks later, and by mid-June 1935, Hunter and Karpis had arrived in Hot Springs by car. The boys decided to rent a cabin on Lake Hamilton, located only about eight miles from Hot Springs.

While at Lake Hamilton, Hunter recalled that he and Karpis visited a prostitution house located at 1338 Central Avenue. The popular brothel was managed by Grace Goldstein. A peroxide blonde in her late twenties, Goldstein's real name was Jewell LaVerne Grayson. She had a place where Karpis and Hunter could lie low following their robbery of the Erie train.[190] As a matter of fact, Madam Goldstein entertained

Garrettsville Train Depot (library reference date October 22, 1964). *From The Cleveland Press Collection, Michael Schwartz Library, Cleveland State University.*

all the top crooks in Hot Springs, including cops and politicians. Karpis described Goldstein as a "genuine big-leaguer" who was "also hot stuff in bed," and he claimed that "she helped [him] out in a dozen other ways."[191] Goldstein aided Karpis in maintaining great connections. And as a fugitive from the law, Karpis appeared to be in great hands. As far as Hunter knew, Karpis did not fraternize with any of the girls except Goldstein, and Hunter hooked up with an eighteen-year-old young lady whose alias was Connie Morris (born Ruth Hamm Robison). Morris reportedly "filled up dates" at Goldstein's place until the end of June 1935. Soon afterward, Morris took up residency with her new beau, Freddie Hunter. Morris later testified that she only knew Karpis and Hunter as brothers Harold and Ed King.[192]

By July 1935, the pressing hunt for Karpis, charged by the Justice Department, had surpassed the twenty-two-month mark. Karpis seemed to just vanish into thin air after agents followed a trail of stolen automobiles through Pennsylvania, Ohio and into the Great Lakes region."[193]

Once returning to Toledo from Hot Springs, Karpis traveled to Cleveland in the fall of 1935, taking two more men into his planned train caper. The first was twenty-one-year-old Milton Lett, referred to as "The Kid," who swept floors at the Harvard Club. The second was a steelworker and family man named Clayton Hall, whose home was just outside Youngtown. Karpis and Hunter remained in the company of Clayton Hall at his home on Ridgewood Drive after word arrived that the FBI was keeping a close eye on Edith Barry's rooming house.[194]

While Karpis was tying up loose ends, Hunter returned to Tulsa, where he solicited the aid of John Brock. Brock agreed to participate in this train heist, and as a result, he and Hunter traveled by train from Tulsa to Cleveland. The following day, the two of them proceeded to Edith Barry's Toledo hideout. It was Edith Barry, the forty-five-year-old rooming house operator, who furnished Karpis and his associates with her rooming house for a short time on November 5, 1935. The gang revisited Barry's house specifically for the purpose of finalizing the plans for the Garrettsville train caper.[195]

The plans for the train heist seemed to be falling into place. Joe Roscoe arranged contact between Karpis and pilot John Zetzer at the Port Clinton, Ohio airport. By the first few days of November 1935, Hunter and Karpis felt comfortable enough to contact Zetzer in person. Zetzer was a former Prohibition rumrunner and no stranger to corruption. The boys wanted to charter an airplane for a trip to the South, and Zetzer seemed like the man for the job.

Just as things seemed to be coming together, and just two days before the train caper, Sam Coker was carted off to the hospital. Coker was supposed to serve as a spy at the Cleveland depot, making sure the payroll money was on the train and that the FBI hadn't caught on. As Karpis described, Coker had "latched onto a dirty whore and came down with more than gonorrhea" after attempting to rid his body of the disease by injecting a solution of iodine. The day before the heist, Coker was still confined at the Mercy Hospital in Toledo. Karpis attempted to replace Coker, but after rejecting a number of possible substitutes, he decided to take a chance and abandon that part of the plan.[196]

On November 6, 1935, Hunter and Karpis visited Zetzer at Port Clinton and gave him $100 toward the purchase of their getaway Stinson airplane. The boys made arrangements to meet up with Zetzer again at the airport garage on the evening of November 7.[197]

As the new kid on the block, Brock recalled that during the late afternoon of November 6, 1935, the gang discussed what each man's part was to be in the train robbery. Groves, as the oldest and more experienced, was the best person to overtake an unassuming train engineer and fireman while Karpis and Campbell entered the baggage and mail car. Freddie Hunter was to stand out on the platform and take a general view of everybody, and Hunter was to take care of the express man. This part of the plan was somewhat revised, according to Karpis, and Hunter ultimately had the chore of covering the parking lot. Karpis wanted to make sure that nobody drove out of the place or left the station platform. Karpis emphasized that he, Campbell and Brock would take the train—with Karpis in the feature role of heisting the money from the payroll car.[198]

After finalizing their strategy, Karpis informed Brock that Freddie Hunter would take him out to the Clyde Rochat farmhouse on Rural Route 5 near Newton Falls, Ohio, to spend the night. Hunter would then travel into Youngstown to retrieve the getaway car. Campbell and Groves would also spend the night at the farm, and arrangements would be made with Rochat to take all three men out to meet up with Karpis and Hunter the following day. Hunter had known Rochat for a number of years, and he knew he could firmly rely on his friend.[199]

In his testimony, Rochat explained that he became acquainted with Freddie Hunter about fifteen years earlier while Hunter was living in Warren, Ohio. According to Rochat, Hunter lived with Rochat and his wife, Amanda, at their home in Leavittsburg during 1932 and 1933. This was the period shortly after Freddie was released from the Ohio State Penitentiary. Given his ties to Hunter, Rochat was familiar with Karpis and able to identify a photo of him as the man whom he knew as Ray Miller. Rochat indicated that he was first acquainted with Karpis in February 1935, when the two met concerning Karpis's interest in buying a bird dog. At that time, Karpis told Rochat that he was a representative of the Standard Oil Company and was working in the Warren and Youngstown territory.

Karpis and Campbell had previously visited the Rochat home several times together. Around October 15, 1935, Rochat and his wife moved to their new home in Newton Falls, Ohio (also Trumbull County).[200] On November 6, 1935, the night before the train heist, Rochat reported that Karpis arrived at his home around 11:00 p.m. with a tall and slender gentleman, whom he later identified as John Brock from a photograph. Karpis told Rochat that Brock would be staying overnight along with Harry Campbell and Benson Groves. Before wrapping up the conversation, Karpis reminded Rochat to bring the three men to the place known as Four Corners (about two miles from the Rochat farm) early the next afternoon.[201]

For folks who know Portage County and the northeastern area, Four Corners was the area that connected four townships: Ravenna, Rootstown, Charlestown and Edinburg. Most from the area will nostalgically recall the East Park Restaurant—an eatery and bar that stood for nearly six decades at the intersection of this Four Corners encompassing Routes 5, 14, 44 and 59 (Main Street).

The inconspicuous Rochat farmhouse, nestled near the wooded area of Newton Falls, is where the majority of the Karpis gang stayed the night. The robbery of the mail train would be the following day.[202] In the early afternoon of November 7, 1935, at about 12:15 p.m., Rochat stated that he returned from his work in the steel mills to his farm. When he arrived, John Brock, Benson Groves and Harry Campbell were anxiously waiting for him. As previously instructed by Karpis, Rochat drove the three men in Harry Campbell's 1934 Ford coupe to the place known as Four Corners. Shortly after Rochat arrived, Karpis and Hunter drove up in a gray 1935 Plymouth sedan. The three men got out of the car Rochat was driving and quickly entered Karpis's gray sedan. Karpis's coupe had a trunk in the rear, and the guns were secured back there. The five men quickly drove off together, headed in a westerly direction toward Garrettsville.

Rochat reported that he never saw those men again and that he kept the Ford coupe at his farm.[203] Supposedly, Harry Campbell told Rocat that he was going to leave the coupe with the farmer and that Rochat was welcome to use it at his leisure.

The five men with their guns drove into Garrettsville and awaited the train's arrival, which was expected at about 2:15 p.m. Karpis recalled that their equipment for the caper included three machine guns, a rifle and five pistols. For reinforcement, Karpis recalled that they took some items that, he noted, they had "rarely" used in the past. These items included two sticks of dynamite, some caps, a fuse and some cigars that Karpis kept in his pocket to set off the dynamite wicks if necessary. The ability to blast their way into the mail car would be necessary in the event that the mail clerks spotted them in advance.[204]

IN WILD WEST FASHION

It reads like a memorable scene from Clint Eastwood's 2011 biographical drama *J. Edgar*. During an interview with the *Cleveland Plain Dealer*, a young man in his late twenties declared, "One time, I told some of my friends that I'd like to be in one of those robberies just to see how it felt. But, believe me, I've had enough…I can still feel that machine gun in my back."[205] On that fateful day of November 7, 1935, Earl N. Davis, a young news agent from Garrettsville, was picking up the afternoon *Cleveland Press* at the Garrettsville train depot. Little did he know that he would become an involuntary aid to five outlaws.

Carried out in American Wild West fashion, these robbers—some masked with handkerchiefs—swung into position on the station platform under the terrified gaze of nearly a dozen men and women. Systematically, Karpis and his fellow marauders lined up the petrified victims. Aided by the muzzle of a machine gun, Mr. Davis, who was exhausted from holding his arms up, was ordered to carry four heavy mail pouches from the platform to the bandits' Plymouth sedan.[206] As he was loading the pouches into the car, Davis noticed the weapons on the seat. Not for one second did this family man contemplate playing the hero by seizing one of those guns.

There are some old-timers from the Garrettsville area who have spoken in great detail about their firsthand recollections of this last criminal act by Public Enemy No. 1. Dr. Myron Thomas, at the time of the train heist, was just a boy about five years old whose home sat within clear view of the depot. Along with his mother, Thomas watched this robbery take place from the front window of his house. In his retelling of the events, Dr. Thomas stated somewhat humorously in a letter dated May 3, 2014:

Garrettsville Train Depot and the site of the November 7, 1935 train caper pulled off by Karpis. *From James A. Garfield Historical Society (photo dated November 9, 1935, by the* Cleveland Press).

I remember the engineer and fireman being pulled out of the engine [compartment], *and a lot of commotion in the area. My mother called my father at his office, which was over the Pelsue Drug Store. At that time, the only law enforcement in town was a night watchman. She* [Thomas's mother] *then had the telephone operators connect her with the Sheriff's Office in Ravenna who were really too far away to do much. They suggested that she shoot at the escape car to mark it so that it could be identified later. Since there were Tommy guns sticking out of every window* [of the getaway car] *as the car drove away, I think that she wisely declined their suggestion. I was hiding behind a cast-iron radiator and that would be of little value if the Tommy guns opened up.*

I believe the robbers stayed that night in Windham on a farm worked by an Indian named Brochette [Clyde Rochat as reported in the FBI records]. *I think that he was the father of Karpas'* [sic] *girlfriend in St. Paul, Minnesota named Brochette. At that time, St. Paul's mayor declared that St. Paul was an open city to gangsters as long as they made no trouble in the city.*

Garrettsville Train and Freight Depots, 1910. *Author's private collection.*

John Brock later described a scene where Freddie Hunter had tied a handkerchief over his face during the robbery while Benson Groves donned a false mustache, one of those long droopy jobs. Groves's long strip of artificial hair above his lip was reminiscent of those worn by western actors in the silent movies of the 1920s. Convinced that he might be identified, Groves rubbed rouge on his cheeks and chin. Karpis remarked in his memoirs that Groves looked so out of sorts that he was afraid Groves was going to "scare the hell out of" folks. As the robbery commenced, Karpis couldn't help but be distracted by two repairmen perched up on a telephone pole. The repairmen's gaze was fixated in Groves's direction; they were pointing while laughing hysterically.

Struggling for a response to the repairmen's uncontrollable laughter, Karpis heard the train whistle and instantly jumped into action. Wearing a sort of throwaway topcoat with one of the pockets ripped open, Karpis was concealing a machinegun with a twenty-shot clip on a strap slung over his shoulder. Brock was standing in the middle of the station's platform trying to look tough with his tommy gun, though likely failed miserably.[207]

When the train stopped and the doors to the mail car swung open, Karpis leveled his machine gun at the two clerks staring in amazement at the outlaw. To Karpis's utter shock, the clerks slammed the mail car doors shut and hid. After throwing a stick of unlit dynamite through the mail car window and then threatening to cast in a second stick with the wick lit, Karpis began to count down from five. Karpis only had to reach four before the doors swung back open. Once those doors were wide open, three clerks appeared. Karpis described the third clerk as a "big, heavy-set Negro." Karpis hadn't noticed that third clerk before but characterized him with agitation as "a nervy son of a bitch." "You can't do this, man," he insisted to Karpis. "Get off with that gun."

Not one of the three clerks raised his hands in submission until Karpis tried to fire a warning shot over their heads. The gun didn't go off, but Karpis claimed that the sound of the hammer falling startled the men. Seized with fear, the clerks' hands instantly reached for the sky.

Staring fixedly at the mail bags stacked from the floor to ceiling, Karpis took a mental tally. After securing the payroll bag for Warren, Karpis demanded the one for Youngstown. "It isn't on here," the old clerk answered. Dear God! It seemed the Youngstown payroll had been shipped out the previous day. In disbelief, Karpis decried, "Look out Harry, I'm going to shoot this guy." Karpis was mad enough to pull the trigger, and a single discharge from a gun produced a visible flash.

It wasn't Karpis who fired off that shot, although he attempted. The ballistics evidence secured from the postal inspectors proved that Harry Campbell fired his gun. In the heat of perpetrating the robbery, Harry fired a shot into the mail car, and the bullet ricocheted and struck one of the mail custodians. Fortunately, the bullet was deflected by the steel-framed top of the mail cab, preventing serious injury to the mail clerk.[208]

Despite some of the hiccups during the train robbery, Karpis's criminal acuity was on point when it came to the successful heist of Erie train no. 626. Though somewhat disappointing, these outlaws escaped with $34,000 in cash and $11,650 in bond securities (modern-day equivalent of nearly $715,000).[209] The heist went off without any delays, and the bandits quickly escaped the unsuspecting village of Garrettsville in their Plymouth sedan. But as the bandits' car sped away, witnesses noted the license plate number. C.P. Morrow, a Garrettsville coal dealer, trailed the thieves' car part of the way. At Freedom Station (later known as Cain's Garage and located opposite State Route 700), Morrow lost track of the robbers, who turned onto State Route 88 and headed south toward Ravenna (Portage County).[210]

Many decades after the train robbery, Claudia Garrett (Freedom Township native) told an exhilarating story:

> *The day of the great train robbery, my great-grandmother, Bernice Younker Hitchcock Crew, was outside on the Hitchcock Crew Farm located on Freedom Road* [also known as Old 700 or State Route 700 when it crossed State Route 88] *in sight of the Freedom Train Station. She said she became alarmed by a car that came roaring down Freedom Road, heading south past the Freedom Station with men in the car. She watched the car cross the tracks and head south towards Charlestown. It was a car she had never seen before. In those days, everyone knew the make and model of their neighbors' cars so any car they didn't recognize really stood out.*
>
> *Before the arsenal, Freedom Road (old 700) would have been a direct route south out of our area, with major roads off of it along the way and leading to bigger towns and cities. When the family heard about the train robbery and "Creepy Al," they always wondered if that was the gang roaring away with the loot from the train robbery!*[211]

Erie train no. 626 proceeded eastwardly from the Garrettsville Depot until it reached the final destination of Pittsburgh.

FIGHT OR FLIGHT

After making their great escape from Garrettsville, Karpis and his company of villains traveled over many rough and relentless back roads. At about seven o'clock that evening, the gang met up with Joe Roscoe about seven miles out of Port Clinton. They cautiously followed Roscoe into a garage burrowed within the picturesque town of Port Clinton, Ohio. Brock reported that the occupants of the two cars were able to recognize one another through a prearranged signal of flashing their headlights on and off.[212]

Port Clinton was a location on the North Coast of Lake Erie where visitors could walk the sandy beaches of the area's coastline. The garage at Port Clinton was on the edge of the historic downtown, which remains today near Put-in-Bay located on South Bass Island. The Port Clinton garage, sharing space with a small airport, housed a big building with huge double doors in front and a little office built into one corner. A towering stove stood just outside the office. The boys quickly carried the mail bags into the office and ripped them open with the greatest anticipation one could imagine. Those present during this unveiling included Karpis, Harry Campbell, Freddie Hunter and Brock himself. Joe Roscoe and the garage man were standing around the stove in the garage, given that it was usually cold weather during mid-autumn in northeastern Ohio. The $34,000 in cash was taken from the bags, and the bags and the remainder of their contents were burned in the stove.

The money was split up by Karpis, with expenses being taken out beforehand: $6,000 went to Joe Roscoe, $5,000 of which was money that Roscoe had advanced to the gang to finance the train robbery. The remaining $1,000 went to Roscoe for leading the gang to the garage and for the use of the garage. The pilot, John Zetzer, received $1,000 for disposing of the evidence and for the purchase of the Plymouth coupe used in the robbery. Zetzer later disposed of the Plymouth in Lake Erie. Zetzer also received another $1,500 for the purchase of the Stinson aircraft and for trips

1930s pilot John Zetzer of Port Clinton, Ohio (undated). *Ottawa County Historical Society & Museum (Ohio).*

to Hot Springs, Arkansas, and Tulsa, Oklahoma. Furthermore, $5,100 was awarded to each of the five actual participants, and an unknown share was reserved for Sam Coker, who was supposed to have been in on the job but was sick due to his serious diagnosis of "gonorrheal rheumatism."[213]

A discussion followed between the men about leaving Port Clinton, and Karpis asked Campbell if he was headed down south along with him and Brock. Campbell replied with great relief that he was returning home to Toledo. Campbell had a wife waiting for him there. Campbell's gal Wynona Burdette became a fling of his past after she and Dolores Delaney were captured by Bureau agents. Campbell, Groves (alias Grayson) and Roscoe left the garage around 11:00 p.m. in Roscoe's car and headed for Toledo.

After Roscoe and the others left the garage, Brock, Karpis and Hunter traveled about ten or twelve blocks to the home of John Zetzer, who resided on Laurel Avenue in Port Clinton. The boys stayed the night at the Zetzer home. They all slept in the front bedroom at the house. No dummies, they had the guns with them in their handbags. At about 10:00 a.m. the next morning, the boys took off from a field just outside of town in the airplane piloted by Zetzer. The flight headed south toward Hot Springs, and all seemed to be going well in their efforts to avoid apprehension. Brock would continue on to Oklahoma.[214]

After two forced landings and spending one night sleeping under the stars, the pilot and anxious passengers finally arrived in Hot Springs. Before landing, Karpis instructed Brock to give Zetzer an additional $500 once he reached Oklahoma. Karpis and Hunter reached their destination in Hot Springs, and Brock continued on to Tulsa. Because of another forced landing, Brock did not reach his destination until the next day.[215] Shortly after putting his feet on the pavement at the airport, Brock reconnected with his old associate, George "Burrhead" Keady.

CHAPTER 14

"CLOAK AND DAGGER"

The Waiting Game

Immediately following the Garrettsville train heist, witnesses interviewed by the postal inspectors reported that they "identified a photograph of Alvin Karpis as the leader of the gang." As previously mentioned, the postal inspectors became engaged in the investigation as $11,650 in bonds belonging to the postal service was robbed. Further investigation and information revealed through a confidential informant (secured by the City of Tulsa postal inspector) noted that Sam Coker left Tulsa shortly before the train robbery. Coker indicated that he was going to participate in a mail robbery. A second informant in Tulsa indicated that John Brock took Sam Coker's place.[216]

It wasn't until the first part of December 1935 that Sam Coker finally recovered from his medical indiscretion and made it back from Toledo. Once he returned, Coker contacted John Brock at the Lincoln Hotel, and Brock was relieved to hear from Coker that the rest of the boys were all right. Brock excitedly informed "Burrhead" Keady about the money he made up north. He relinquished those "earnings" to Keady for safekeeping. But in no time at all, the police raided Herford's gambling place, where Keady had Brock's money tucked away.

The confessions provided by Sam Coker and George "Burrhead" Keady revealed John Brock's complicity in the train heist. The worst had happened once Brock's money was confiscated by the police. Further investigation revealed that Brock's pillage, amounting to $3,200 and contained in a sack consisting of mostly $20 bills, was traced back to the Federal Reserve Bank in Cleveland. Brock's photograph was rushed to Cleveland, where post office inspectors exhibited it to witnesses of the Garrettsville train robbery. Still hiding out in Tulsa, Brock was promptly apprehended by the post office officials and brought back to the United States Marshal's Office in Youngstown, Ohio.[217]

Brock's apprehension resulted in a full confession of his complicity in the Garrettsville train robbery. In his admission, Brock stated that he substituted for Sam Coker. Brock also told the postal inspectors that Karpis likely came to Cleveland and made contact with a former prizefighter whose name was unknown. Although Brock didn't know the name of this Karpis contact, he indicated that this individual worked at the Harvard Club just outside the city of Cleveland. This same individual also traveled to Toledo and contacted Joe Roscoe in Canton, giving him the messages of the gang. In turn, contacts with Roscoe were made through the madam Edith Barry, who was in constant and direct contact with the boys.

The prizefighter was later identified as "Smokey" Sharkey, whose true name was John Francis Gorman. As a hired hand, Gorman was a trusted employee of the Harvard Club and in close association with Arthur Hebebrand. Gorman acted as a messenger for Hebebrand, as well as for Harry Campbell and Karpis.[218] Brock indicated that if things got "heated" in Hot Springs, it was likely that Karpis and Hunter would return to Cleveland or Toledo.[219]

During the cold and raw winter months of 1935 and early 1936, the Bureau's pursuit of Karpis followed a pattern of nothing of consequence to report. Special agents spent much of their time chasing small leads or "loafing," remarked Special Agent Thomas McDade. When not entangled in one of those highly anticipated shootouts, agents were sitting around the office, taking in drinks or movies, and many agents frequented the nightclubs and gambling resorts. Agent McDade recorded in his journal that he and Agent Tillman went out to dinner, a ten-cent movie and then on to a burlesque, which McDade described as "terrible."[220]

Initially, Special Agent Earl Connelley appeared to ignore the information obtained by the postal inspectors.[221] In fact, Agent Connelley stated that he "did not believe" that the postal inspectors had "half as much as they would have you believe."[222]

With Karpis's underworld and law enforcement contacts, it is no surprise that this Public Enemy remained on the run for so long. His unsuccessful capture was a feat that inflamed Hoover's sensibilities. As the declared leader and brains of the gang, Hoover referred to Karpis as a "rat." Obviously, this infuriated Karpis. Throughout the Bureau's hunt for Karpis, it had been reported that Karpis's hatred of Hoover resulted in the outlaw sending Hoover a death threat letter. Reportedly, Karpis stated that he intended to kill Hoover as vengeance for the shooting deaths of Ma and Freddie Barker in Florida.[223]

Making matters difficult for Karpis while he was in hiding, during the summer of 1935, Ohio newspapers reported that Hoover claimed he had received a death threat from Karpis in a letter sent from an Ohio town.[224] On the contrary, a letter dated October 24, 1994, and addressed to J. Kevin O'Brien, chief of the Freedom of Information Privacy Section (representing the FBI), stated that a search of the central FBI records produced no such death threat letter from Karpis to Hoover between 1932 and 1936.[225] According to Karpis in his first autobiography, the death threat was a rumor started by Hoover himself.

As the investigations progressed, the postal inspectors reported their evidence to the FBI, and the Bureau was compelled to compete for jurisdiction in this investigation.[226] It was crime historian Bryan Burrough who concluded that "as a result of the Cleveland train's payroll delivery being intercepted before it was picked up by the post office in Youngstown, it became the Youngstown Postal Inspectors' jurisdiction."[227]

Despite Karpis's highly debated fingerprint removal, his involvement in the train robbery was identified by one of his prints left behind. The print was lifted from the windowsill of the mail train by postal inspectors. As a result, Special Agent-in-Charge Earl J. Connelley required the Cleveland field office to investigate.[228] Months before, Hoover himself stated that at the moment Karpis had robbed the train, they had no serious leads on his whereabouts.[229] As federal postal inspectors in Youngstown pursued Karpis and his accomplices, they were quickly able to identify the gangsters' prints through a centralized repository of fingerprints established within the Identification Division of the FBI. This repository had also been provided to local police departments since 1924.[230]

Additional evidence presented by the postal inspectors, along with that of the local police, proved that eight men and two women witnessed the train robbery. With the help of these witnesses, it took the postal inspectors only twenty-four hours to pinpoint Karpis and Harry Campbell for the train robbery. Eyewitnesses were able to identify the photos of both men.[231]

Much of the FBI's lethargic response to the initial investigation was attributed to the dismissive behavior of Special Agent Earl J. Connelley. As reported in the official records, Agent Connelley told Assistant Director Ed

Tamm that with the "major trials to prepare for and more," the Bureau was not spending much time looking for Karpis. Since no sightings of Karpis had been reported for more than six months, Karpis was not a priority. It was nearly March of 1936 before the FBI began a full-throttle search.[232]

During its initial investigation, the FBI interviewed Sylvester J. Hettrick, the post office inspector stationed at Cleveland. Inspector Hettrick provided the names and addresses of all the victims of the train heist. The list of victims included various locals, including Mrs. W.L. Scott, Fred R. Ball, Earl N. Davis, Robert Brockett, Frances Brockett, Mrs. E.A. Meadows, Mrs. Thomas (doctor's wife) and W.D. Moses (station agent), all from Garrettsville, Ohio.[233]

Richard Davis indicated that his father, Earl, the victimized news agent from Garrettsville, was picked up without warning by lawmen in the middle of the night and taken to Cleveland to identify possible suspects in a lineup. These suspects were immediately captured on the evening of November 8, 1935. These men were then held in Cleveland in an effort to link them with the automobile used by the robbers. The car bore a license issued in Cleveland that was traced to an empty rental home on the east side. The license eventually led police detectives to Hough Avenue to an apartment in Cleveland occupied by ex-convict Milton Lett.[234]

During the course of the postal inspectors' investigation, it was also learned that Lett had purchased a 1935 gun-metal gray Plymouth sedan under the alias of Thomas J. Shaw. The vehicle was purchased from the Knowles Brown Motor Company in Cleveland in late October 1935 for $740 in cash. This was determined to be the same vehicle used in the train robbery.[235]

The man who purchased this vehicle gave the name of Carl Baker but was later identified to be Thomas J. Shaw. In reality, Mr. Shaw was Milton Lett, a former associate of Harry Campbell who had been employed at the Harvard Club.[236] This was the first clue that incriminated Milton Lett, associating him with the train robbery.[237] The second man identified was the middle-aged Clayton Hall. After threats of prosecution, both Lett and Hall agreed to report directly to the Cleveland Bureau as confidential informants. A familiar story, Karpis's status as Public Enemy No. 1 was not known by either Lett or Hall. Both men testified that they had only known Karpis by the name Ray Miller, a gambler from Cleveland.[238]

Claiming to be in the dark about Karpis's identity, it was during Hall's stay in Hot Springs in January 1936 that he realized that Ray Miller was actually Alvin Karpis. Hall read a story in the *Red Book* magazine by Melvin

Purvis and saw the picture of the Public Enemy who resembled the man he thought was Ray Miller. Hall returned to Youngstown by railroad several days later.[239] While under close scrutiny by the postal inspectors, the FBI initially failed to regard Hall as a person of interest.

While held by the Youngstown Postal Inspectors, John Brock not only admitted his own guilt in the train heist but also identified Karpis, Hunter and Campbell as participants in the train robbery as well. Moreover, Brock offered information on the gang's traditional hideout at Edith Barry's house and the plane trip from Port Clinton to Arkansas.[240] Correspondingly, the postal inspectors were able to find someone at the Port Clinton airport to identify Freddie Hunter's picture. There was tremendous incentive for Brock to tell everything that he knew since U.S. Attorney General Homer Cummings guaranteed a $5,000 reward to anyone who had information about Karpis's whereabouts. The post office inspectors offered another $2,000 for each of these men named in the warrants.[241]

The forty-three-year-old Brock was sentenced by federal judge Paul Jones in a Cleveland courtroom. Brock got off easy, as the postal inspectors informed the court that his cooperation enabled the government to apprehend and convict twelve other persons involved in the train caper. Brock admitted that he passed the mail bags from the train while the other members of the gang covered the train crew.[242]

Once again, Karpis had slipped through the detection of the FBI. In late March 1936, Karpis rented an apartment at 3300 St. Charles Avenue in New Orleans, but he had spent most of his free time and taken most of his meals with Freddie Hunter and his gal, Connie Morris, at their 3343 Canal Street apartment.[243]

By March 25, 1936, FBI agent E.J. Wynn had met with informant Clayton Hall at his home in Youngstown, and Hall identified the photos of Karpis and Hunter as the men who had visited him in January 1936.[244] Facing prosecution by postal inspectors, Hall agreed to help officials locate Karpis—but only if Hall could provide the details in the presence of an FBI agent.[245] Reluctantly, Youngstown postal inspector Sylvester Hettrick permitted Agent Connelley to spend several hours interviewing Hall. Clayton Hall reported to Connelley everything he knew, including the location of Karpis's rental house seven miles south of Hot Springs.

On March 30, 1936, Agent Connelley along with twelve of his agents, twenty other law enforcement officers and several postal inspectors were prepping themselves for a drawn-out gun battle. Since Hall had provided a detailed map of the property where Hunter and Karpis were thought to be residing, these officers had no second thoughts about shooting the place to pieces. They even fired several flares through the windows, with one landing on a bed and igniting a fire. When the agents busted in to put out the fire, they realized—to their dismay—that the house was abandoned.

Karpis and Hunter had been gone for four days. The owner of the home, Mr. Woodcock, was infuriated by the Bureau's negligence. And to add insult to injury, Woodcock was a close friend of Arkansas Democrat Senator Joseph Taylor Robinson. Woodcock made certain that Senator Robinson was aware of the FBI's negligence in shooting up his home, and by all means, Woodcock wanted restitution.[246]

Long gone, Karpis was once again tipped off by the local police in Hot Springs. Karpis was aware that the FBI was closing in on him and fled in plenty of time. He explained, "It was possible to buy off anyone as long as you come up with enough dough."[247] The citizens of Hot Springs confirmed that they had seen Karpis with the chief of police on many occasions.[248] The heat was on, and the Bureau needed to expand its growing network of informants. The agency needed informants who could be motivated by money—or, better yet, find molls who were willing to provide information because of their desperate circumstances.[249] Being so close to these gangsters, molls were women who revealed valuable information when they were most vulnerable or exhausted from living a fugitive life. But getting a moll to talk required strong persuasion or tactics of harsh interrogation.

Chapter 15

HOOVER'S FLEDGLING CAREER

We [the FBI] *are a fact-gathering organization only.*
We don't clear anybody. We don't condemn anybody.
—J. Edgar Hoover

As reported in *Newsweek*, crime had spiked by mid-1935, hence Hoover's request for $5 million in funding came under scrutiny from the Congressional Appropriations Committee. According to Hoover, this additional funding was necessary for the continuation of the FBI's war on crime and twice the amount of Hoover's current budget.[250]

Had Karpis been captured during the March raid in Hot Springs, Hoover would have been spared the heavy criticism he received from Senator Kenneth D. McKellar of Tennessee. McKellar, a Democrat, had been in the Senate since 1926 and was chairman of the subcommittee that oversaw the appropriations of the Department of Justice. McKellar was not the man for Hoover to offend. As the records show, Hoover did indeed offend Senator McKellar around 1933 when Hoover refused to appoint a number of McKellar's constituents as special agents within the Bureau. When McKellar brought this offense to the attention of U.S. Attorney General Homer Cummings, Hoover fired three special agents from McKellar's district.[251] McKellar would not forget this slight.

On April 11, 1936, Hoover arrived on Capitol Hill accompanied by Clyde Tolson, the associate director and Hoover's right-hand man. Hoover believed that he was well prepared. Recent statistics confirmed that his special agents had nearly exterminated kidnapping in the United States since the kidnapping statutes had been enacted in 1932. To add to his impressive

Attorney General Homer Cummings and Hoover, undated. *Author's private collection.*

résumé, Hoover reported that federal bank robbery had been dramatically reduced. To Hoover's credit, the dangerous midwestern criminals had all been killed or captured, except for one: Alvin "Creepy" Karpis, whom the director failed to mention.[252]

During the appropriations hearing, Hoover was prompted with the big question: What were Hoover's qualifications for his job? McKellar had to dig deeper: "So whatever you know about [crime] you learned there in the Department?"

Hoover maintained his composure, nearly reverting to stuttering, but answered, "I learned first-hand; yes sir."

McKellar demanded, "Did you ever make an arrest?"

Hoover responded almost politely, "No sir, I have made investigations."

McKellar pressed further with certain vindictiveness, "How many arrests have you made, and who were they?"

Hoover went into some detail and answered in a similar manner with which he handled his investigations, including a narrative of the case of Ludwig Martens, the former Bolshevik ambassador to the United States.

McKellar again pursued, "Did you make the arrests?"

Hoover confidently stated, "The arrests were made by the immigration officers under my supervision."

To this, McKellar drove his point home, "I am talking about the actual arrests.…You never arrested them, actually?"

McKellar forcefully prodded until he achieved his desired outcome: America's top G-Man had never made an arrest. According to one biographer, Hoover felt "that his manhood had been impugned."[253] After returning to his headquarters following the hearing, Hoover was committed to, if not obsessed with, making Karpis his first arrest.

By the second week in April 1936, Karpis and Grace Goldstein made it back to New Orleans.[254] Meanwhile, the agents who remained in Hot Springs were continually told by their contacts that Goldstein was intimately connected to Karpis. Knowledge that fishing occupied the majority of Karpis's pastime had been acquired; therefore, many of the Bureau's agents had gone undercover as fishermen or tourists.[255]

Subsequently, informant Clayton Hall was convinced that Goldstein would confide in him if he contacted her. Under the thumb of Agent Connelley, Hall arrived at a tourist camp in Hot Springs escorted by one of the Bureau's agents. Hall and the agents anxiously awaited Karpis in the tourist camp.

Karpis was not relaxing at a tourist camp in Hot Springs. Karpis and Goldstein were vacationing in Florida and Biloxi. When Karpis ferried Goldstein back to her brothel in Hot Springs, the FBI was waiting for her.[256]

While the FBI anticipated Goldstein's arrival, it also kept a close eye on the postal inspectors who were swarming about town. In an effort to remove the inspectors from Hot Springs, one of the agents was instructed to create a ruse.

Somehow the FBI's deception was successful, as all the postal inspectors fled Hot Springs, leaving the hunt for Karpis solely in the hands of the Bureau.[257] To this day, the details surrounding this strategy to move the postal inspectors out of Hot Springs remains undisclosed in FBI files.

After Goldstein returned to the Hatterie Hotel, Clayton Hall was sent in to filter out information. He and Grace talked for hours, and she confided in Hall that Karpis and Hunter were now renting apartments somewhere in New Orleans. Yet Goldstein told Hall that she didn't know the exact location of Karpis's apartment.

Although they remained inconspicuous, the outlaws' troubles were mounting. It was April 27, 1936, and Hunter and Karpis were listening to the radio at Hunter's apartment when a news flash was broadcast. Now the whole country was privy to the fact that Karpis, Hunter and Campbell were wanted by the Post Office Department for their involvement in America's last great train heist. Not particularly bothered by the news, Karpis left the next morning for Mississippi on a fishing trip, and Hunter claimed that he did not see Karpis again until the morning of May 1 and back at Hunter's apartment.[258]

With Clayton Hall's helpful revelation, Agent Connelley arrived in New Orleans on April 27. The resolute agent-in-charge decided to take Grace Goldstein into custody to interrogate her about Karpis's location, but Goldstein refused to give Karpis's address. The FBI believed it was forced to take serious action by tracking down Goldstein's family in East Texas. The agents gave their tough talk and convinced the family that Goldstein could be indicted for harboring Karpis. Two days later, Goldstein agreed to provide Karpis's address, but only to Connelley and only if the FBI promised not to prosecute anyone in her family. Coincidentally, Goldstein didn't even know Karpis's address, but she knew Hunter's apartment location and that Karpis ate most of his meals there.

Hot on the heels of Karpis, Hoover wasted no time securing a charter flight, arriving in New Orleans on the evening of April 30.[259] On the morning of May 1, 1936, Karpis had just returned from Mississippi after his fishing expedition and after surveying a few possible sites for "the taking." Karpis was eyeing a prospective train heist and a big construction project called Pickwick Dam, which had a good-sized payroll.[260] By the time the afternoon rolled around, Karpis had arrived at Freddie's apartment on the corner of Canal Street and Jefferson Davis Parkway. Within a short while, Karpis and Hunter would be leaving to pick up Karpis's car at a nearby service garage. Two parked cars sat across the intersection of Canal Street. Agents Connelley and Clarence Hurt, a short and stocky thirty-nine-year-old G-Man with a receding hairline, were in the lead car. Hoover, Clyde Tolson and two other agents were directly behind them.[261]

CHAPTER 16

"THE STORY OF HOOVER THE HERO IS FALSE"

The highly anticipated capture of Alvin "Creepy" Karpis was not the exact scene depicted in Clint Eastwood's biopic *J. Edgar.* The G-Men had strategically taken their positions, but not on a busy street within the city of New Orleans, with Hoover willing to risk his very life to give Congress what it wanted: an "armed American hero." And Karpis surely didn't step out of his Plymouth coupe and declare, "Mr. Hoover himself, I'm gonna be famous!" Yet Hoover's presence at Karpis's capture would make "Creepy" prominent among gangsters of the era.

Rather, this was the scene. It was a steamy eighty-seven degrees in New Orleans around 5:30 p.m. on May 1, 1936. In a busy suburb of New Orleans, Freddie Hunter's coupe was parked inconspicuously on Canal Street. Identified by a Louisiana license plate, the car was about to be entered by the last of the most notorious criminals of the 1930s, Alvin "Creepy" Karpis, and his criminal sidekick Freddie Hunter. Karpis had just entered the car. The boys were personally unarmed and entirely oblivious to the ensuing raid.

Agents Hurt and Connelley rushed to cross Canal Street and blocked Hunter's car. Out jumped Hurt and Connelley, who promptly covered the outlaws with their guns. Karpis was seated in front of the steering wheel, and Hunter was just getting into the passenger's seat. Being the tough guy that he was, Agent Hurt wasted no time in leveling his .351-caliber Winchester rifle in Karpis's face through the car's window. As Hurt and Connelley covered Karpis from the front, the automobile containing

Hoover and Clyde Tolson came barreling across Canal Street to block the rear of Hunter's Plymouth and provide additional gun cover.[262]

Hoover later recounted that out of the second car he jumped, and he and Tolson led Agents Brantley and Buchanan to Karpis and Hunter.[263] This advance by Hoover was recorded in a report by Connelley but became highly contested in Karpis's autobiography.[264] It was widely reported that the streets were in chaos as a few dozen G-Men vaulted from every direction.[265] In his own careful analysis, veteran agent Larry Wack reported that there were eighteen G-Men on the scene and not twenty-eight, as has been widely reported by historians and the press throughout the decades.

After being forced from the car, a demanding voice shouted, "Alvin Karpis, you're under arrest!"[266] Karpis admitted that he could feel the rifle stuck in his back with the barrel shaking against his backbone.[267] Karpis described one particular agent as "the cool guy with the machine gun." This "cool guy" was Special Agent W.L. "Buck" Buchanan, who took off his tie and used it to secure Karpis's wrists.[268] Shockingly, not one agent had brought handcuffs that day, as Karpis had often boasted that he would never be taken alive.[269]

Wack confirmed, "We [FBI] also have established that it was the necktie of SA W.L. 'Buck' Buchanan that was used to bind Karpis' hands at the moment."[270]

During a June 1957 interview with Ken Jones, Hoover explained, "We did not expect to take him [Karpis] easily and we planned the raid carefully. Four assistants and I were to enter the front door. The other squads were deployed in the rear and on both sides of the building."

As claimed by Hoover, the signal for action was delayed when a man on a horse moved into the road lane beside the through traffic. They waited until the horseman passed, and then the agents judiciously moved forward. As Hoover and his agents moved, two men stepped from the apartment and walked quickly down the steps. Immediately, the agents recognized Karpis as one of them. As the two men walked toward the car on the curb, a young boy on a bicycle scooted between the two outlaws and Hoover's vantage point. To protect the boy, Hoover stated that he and his agents moved out and hurried forward, demanding the surrender of Karpis and Hunter as they entered their car.

Hoover gloated that Karpis's expression was one of "amazement and fright." Neither Karpis nor Hunter resisted. "The tough hoodlum turned ashen. Like all their breed." Their courage oozes away when on the "other side of a gun," Hoover remarked with his typical confident arrogance.[271]

Various guns were recovered from Hunter's automobile and the house. Newspapers around the country reported that "without firing one shot," the FBI captured this last Public Enemy who remained alive long enough to be taken into custody.[272]

In Hoover's viewpoint, Karpis was especially dangerous because the outlaw was plotting a mass murder of federal agents prior to his capture. Hoover claimed that the murder of these G-Men was to be accomplished with a machine gun ambush in Cleveland. Karpis would lure G-Men to an unnamed street corner and hide in a building nearby. Once the agents arrived, Karpis would open fire on the unwitting lawmen. But Hoover stated that this plot was scrapped in favor of an even more "desperate plan."[273]

A subsequent plot, Hoover revealed, called for the "slaying of Justice Department agents" in Los Angeles, Chicago and New York, as well as, finally, a trip to Washington to kill Mr. Hoover himself—but this plan was foiled.[274] For reasons that Hoover never fully explained, no other evidence of this plot has ever been discussed or discovered.

THE LAST MEN STANDING

Immediately following the capture of Karpis, Hoover held a press conference stating that after "great personal danger," he had secured his first arrest by putting the cuffs on this "cold, calculating" and "nasty sort of individual."[275]

With strong denunciation, Karpis wrote in his autobiography that "the story of Hoover the Hero is false" and a line of "bullshit." When Karpis was first arrested, he stated that "Hoover was nowhere to be seen."[276] In contrast to Karpis's declaration, veteran agent Larry Wack explained, "Karpis did not see Hoover come from behind the apartment building. If anyone lied about what happened, it was Karpis."

In Wack's FBI-supported view of the events, he stated with utmost certainty:

> *Karpis essentially made allegations to embarrass Hoover and the FBI, and attempt[ed] to make a lot of money doing it. His TV interviews would give him the stage he was denied.*
>
> *The media accounts of that day in New Orleans were no doubt exaggerated and care should be taken in using them as official sources of what happened. If readers accept Karpis' accounts as the truth, then it*

must be accepted that most, if not all, of the eighteen (18) FBI agents present that day, including Hoover, outright lied in their official reports on his instructions or those of SAC Connelley. Readers would also have to believe that all eighteen present kept the arrest secret to themselves their entire careers, into retirement, and eventually took them to the grave without mentioning anything to their close FBI friends or family. Not highly likely and an accusation of such is a severe challenge to their integrity.

This "revelation" by Karpis is in direct conflict with SAC E.J. Connelley's very detailed report of where Hoover was, in what car he occupied, and his actions at the scene. It's also in direct conflict with other FBI agents present and their own statements. According to Hoover's own telephone call to FBIHQ, his arrival at the Karpis vehicle the moment of the arrest was delayed by two obstructions; a young boy and a policeman on horseback.[277]

Curt Gentry, Hoover's biographer, claimed that the special agents involved in the capture of Karpis were well aware that the director's story was not exactly what happened, but none of them publicly disputed

The G-Men at the scene of Karpis's capture, including Hoover (*center*), Clyde Tolson (*right*) and Earl J. Connelley (*left*). *Connelley Family Collection.*

this official account.[278] There are no quotes from Hoover or anyone else suggesting that Hoover had been among the first to actually take the men into custody. The reports did not even include the details that emerged later in books, magazines or in Agent Connelley's official memo. The headline term "Hoover Himself" seems to be a "semantic stretch," claimed historian Richard Kudish.[279]

In the end, it did not matter, as the headlines in the *New York Times* read, "Karpis Captured in New Orleans by Hoover Himself."[280] Many accounts, both media and scholarly, claimed that Karpis was the only lawbreaker ever to be personally arrested by J. Edgar Hoover.[281] By the time Karpis was captured by the FBI, he was wanted for fourteen murders, but without hard evidence.

To the Bureau's surprise, it took a mere twenty minutes to bring Karpis into a holding cell at the post office building in New Orleans.[282] Yet capturing Karpis was no easy feat. Even Hoover admitted that Karpis and his "cronies constituted the toughest gang of hoodlums that the FBI [had] been called upon to eliminate."[283]

Karpis and G-Men landing in St. Paul, May 2, 1936. Agent Earl Connelley is dressed in the white suit and standing outside the plane. Karpis was still onboard the plane. *Larry Wack (http://historicalgmen.squarespace.com).*

Karpis arriving in handcuffs at the St. Paul Federal Building, May 2, 1936. See Hoover leading the way in the foreground. *From The Cleveland Press Collection, Michael Schwartz Library, Cleveland State University.*

On May 2, 1936, around 9:45 a.m., Karpis—sullen, travel weary and shivering—was brought back to the frigid temperature of St. Paul to face trial. Escorted personally by Hoover and his hand-picked squad of agents, Karpis landed in St. Paul only twelve hours after the heavily armed party flew northward out of New Orleans. It was reported that during the plane flight, Karpis was "manacled" and harassed. Karpis himself believed that when the plane got up a good distance into the air, Hoover and his agents would just thrust him out of the plane's door.

Upon landing in St. Paul, Hoover divulged additional details of Karpis's capture during a press conference in the federal building. To the dismay of informant John Brock, the top G-Man emphasized that "no reward" would be paid by the FBI to any persons who were seeking the $7,000 price offered for Karpis's arrest.[284] As evidenced by historians and academics, reporters were not invited to witness the FBI's arresting events. Instead, those in the

Karpis arriving at the St. Paul Courthouse accompanied by G-Men. Dwight Brantley (*left*), agent in charge of the Oklahoma City office, and Clarence Hurt, former city police detective, are shown with Karpis. Both aided in the New Orleans raid. *Minnesota State Historical Society and Library.*

media proclaimed that they were given "narratives delivered by Hoover" for which they could reconstruct and circulate the details after the arrests had already been made.[285]

After her son's capture, Anna Karpowicz sued *TIME* magazine for defamation of character when the magazine reported that "Alvin Karpis is a product of Chicago's west side. His mother did time in Kansas, Missouri and Oklahoma prisons." Originally, Mrs. Karpowicz's attorneys had filed a libel suit for $100,000, but she settled with *TIME* for $2,000 only nine months later. The facts proved that Karpis's mother had never been in jail—or, for that matter, had any unlawful offenses.[286]

Despite Karpis's surprise capture, Harry Campbell remained on the run. Campbell admitted that he had married Gertrude Billiter nearly one year before in Bowling Green, Ohio, on May 29, 1935. So, naturally, Campbell felt obligated to stay back in Toledo with his new wife after the train heist.

Gertrude had been well acquainted with Toledo sheriff O'Reilly for some time, and she made sure that the sheriff became acquainted with her new husband. In a statement to officials, Gertrude Billiter claimed that she had no knowledge of her husband's criminality. Later, Campbell voiced his belief that it was Sheriff O'Reilly who identified him to the Bureau as its "wanted man."[287]

With no advance notice to Toledo's city officials, Hoover arrived at Toledo's Transcontinental Airport at 2:00 a.m. accompanied by his heavily armed investigators to arrest Public Enemy No. 2. On May 7, 1936, after a seamless raid of a Toledo apartment, the armed Harry Campbell was pounced on and quickly whisked away by airplane to St. Paul. Once landing, Campbell was interrogated about the kidnapping of Bremer back in 1934. Karpis was also in St. Paul awaiting conviction for the same kidnapping.[288]

One week following the arrests of Karpis and Campbell, U.S. Attorney General Homer Cummings declared that it was "just another illustration of the need for a mobile force such as our Federal Bureau of Investigation in the 'rapid fire capture' of Karpis." Cummings was sure to add that this was a job outside the expertise of local officers.[289] On May 9, 1936, Karpis was charged with the William Hamm kidnapping, and his bail was set at $500,000. This was the largest bail ever set for any criminal in the United States up until that time.[290]

By mid-1936, Attorney General Cummings had greatly diminished the Office of the Attorney General, essentially elevating Hoover to a legendary state.[291] In the depths of the Depression, the number of special agents rose from 353 in 1933 to 658 by 1938.[292]

Karpis and Campbell would not be Hoover's only arrests. According to FBI documents, Hoover made his next-to-last arrest on December 15, 1936, when he captured Harry Brunette of New York. Brunette was wanted for the kidnapping of a state trooper and a string of bank robberies. Hoover's last arrest became an exclusive story provided by Walter Winchell, the award-winning journalist and 1930s broadcaster and gossip columnist. Winchell detailed that Hoover's last arrest had taken place as the legendary lawman was walking through the New York City streets. The event culminated on the corner of Twenty-Eighth Street and Fifth Avenue when the notorious Louis "Lepke" Buchalter unexpectedly surrendered to Hoover on the evening of August 24, 1939. Buchalter was a Jewish American mobster and head of the mafia's hit squad Murder Inc. Buchalter was one of the premier labor racketeers in New York City. After being convicted of murder, Buchalter became the only major mob boss to receive the death penalty.[293]

CHAPTER 17

AND NOW YOU'LL KNOW
THE REST OF THE STORY

Alvin Karpis was charged in St. Paul on July 24, 1936. Before entering his plea, Karpis told Special Agent John Brennan during an interview: "[I] always regarded Harry as being pretty much dumb, and [I] believe if it could be arranged to have Harry Campbell put in an adjoining cell, [I] could give Campbell more advice in five minutes than any lawyer could give him in five years, and what is more, Harry Campbell would follow it."[294]

With Karpis's persuasive coaxing, special agents brought the downtrodden Harry Campbell to visit Karpis at the St. Paul County Jail. During their one-on-one meeting, Karpis told Campbell to plead guilty to the Bremer kidnapping charges, and in turn, Karpis would plead guilty to the charges related to the Hamm kidnapping. This way, Karpis thought, the government would not go to the effort and expense of trying Karpis on the Bremer charge. As Karpis predicted, Harry Campbell agreed to enter a plea of guilty to the indictment charging Campbell with "conspiracy to kidnap Edward G. Bremer."[295]

It was July 27, 1936, while anticipating his own sentencing, that Karpis mustered up enough courage to charge, "Your Honor, I have nothing to say for myself but I would like to say that Mr. [John "Jack"] Peifer is entirely innocent and that ["Byron"] Bolton's testimony is mostly false."

Awaiting his own fate, John "Jack" Peifer, the brainchild of the Hamm kidnapping, was also indicted and convicted in the William Hamm kidnapping case. Peifer always told the gang that he could never survive

Above: Harry Campbell's FBI mug shot, May 7, 1936. *Maryland National Archives*.

RIght: Karpis's official police mug shot after his capture in New Orleans. *From The Cleveland Press Collection, Michael Schwartz Library, Cleveland State University*.

prison. As a result of the evidence presented, Peifer received a thirty-year sentence to be carried out in the Leavenworth Federal Penitentiary. Totally aghast at the severity of his punishment, Peifer took his life after returning to his cell at the Ramsey County Jail. It is believed that Peifer had ingested potassium cyanide.[296]

The judge's sentencing was swift and the punishment fierce with life imprisonment. Two days after receiving their life sentences at the St. Paul Courthouse, Karpis, Charles "Old Fitz" Fitzgerald and Harry Campbell were temporarily committed to Leavenworth, Kansas. Karpis cunningly avoided trial for the Bremer kidnapping by pleading guilty to the earlier Hamm snatch. Both Karpis and the FBI agreed that not one dollar of the $100,000 ransom was ever recovered from the Hamm abduction. The star witness for the government in the Hamm case was Bryan "Byron" Bolton, who issued a complete and detailed confession to the FBI about the Karpis-Barker Gang's kidnapping. Bolton was also the main witness in the Bremer snatch. Despite his witness for the prosecution in the Bremer case, Bolton received a three-year conviction served concurrently, with a similar sentence imposed in connection with the abduction of Hamm.[297]

The decrees of lengthy imprisonment were daunting. Had Karpis been indicted and convicted for the Garrettsville train heist, he would have only received forty years in prison. Interestingly enough, the only psychiatric review to be conducted on Karpis was carried out at the beginning of his incarceration at Leavenworth. The analysis reported the following:

> [Karpis is] *a cold, calculating, socially-irresponsible and indifferent young man who superficially is quiet mannered, unusually polite, and cooperated very well during the interview. Yet, seems the sub-surface mentation of a very dangerous, irresponsible, and cunning social liability. In the opinion of the interviewers, Karpis* [was] *a "constitutional psychopathic inferiority, with criminalistic tendencies."*[298]

At Leavenworth, Karpis kept company with some very dangerous prisoners. He came into immediate contact with an inmate who occupied a cell across the corridor from his solitary confinement. Karpis remarked about the "naked screwball" he witnessed sitting at a table and peering into a microscope. Naked as a jaybird, it startled Karpis when this figure abruptly jumped up from his rickety wooden chair and walked toward the wall of his cell, disappearing like an apparition.

Karpis recalled, "Instantly, I hear what sounds like the singing of thousands of birds rising to a frenzied pitch." There was a curtained doorway between this shadowy man's cell and the next one. The figure soon reappeared with a number of birds perched on his shoulders and a few on his head. To Karpis's surprise, this inmate had nearly two hundred of these birds, all canaries, and all descendants from the two he had started with many years ago.

Karpis and Charles "Old Fitz" Fitzgerald leaving the St. Paul courtroom after sentencing, May 1936. *Courtesy of Robert Ernst*, author of Robbin' Banks and Killin' Cops *(2009)*.

Karpis remembered, "My strange neighbor, standing in the nude decorated with colorful canaries, is Bob Stroud, who has been in isolation here [Leavenworth] for around twenty years." Stroud became famous as the "Birdman of Alcatraz." Oddly enough, Stroud never kept any birds at Alcatraz—only at Leavenworth, where he was incarcerated for murder. Years later, Stroud was given the death penalty for killing a correctional officer in Leavenworth. Robert Stroud's death sentence was later commuted to life imprisonment by President Woodrow Wilson.[299]

As for the fate of the others in Karpis's criminal circle, Edith Barry, the madam who provided refuge for Karpis in Toledo, received a two-year sentence at a federal penitentiary. Criminal pilot John Zetzer received three years at the Northeastern Penitentiary. And two years later, on May 19, 1938, Jewell LaVerne Grayson (alias Grace Goldstein), the Hot Springs madam, was arraigned before the United States commissioner and waived removal, and her bond was set at $10,000. On May 23, 1938, Grayson was removed to the Eastern District of Arkansas.

Jewell LaVerne Grayson (known as Grace Goldstein). The thirty-two-year-old blonde, with hat, is shown leaving a Los Angeles U.S. Marshal's Office after being arrested, May 19, 1938. *Author's private collection.*

Upon her arrival in Little Rock, Grayson was placed under a bond of $10,000 on the indictment for her conspiracy to harbor Karpis and $5,000 on the bond charging her with violation of the White Slave Traffic Act. Grayson reported that while still residing in Hot Springs, she and Karpis were married in New York City on September 25, 1935. Likely in an effort to avoid testifying against Karpis, Grayson claimed that she and the Public Enemy were married under the names of Mr. and Mrs. Ed Woods and lived together in New Orleans as a married couple until Karpis's capture.[300]

Grayson made her bond and was released on June 13, 1938. Despite her unproven claim of marriage to Karpis, a verdict of guilty was returned against Grayson, and she was sentenced to two years in a federal penitentiary. Following in Grayson's footsteps, Ruth Hamm Robison (alias Connie Morris) pled guilty to complicity in harboring Karpis and Hunter. Robison was sentenced to serve one year and one day in a federal penitentiary.[301]

As Karpis's final criminal crony, Freddie Hunter pled guilty to the charge of harboring Karpis. On June 4, 1936, Hunter received two years for harboring a fugitive and was committed to the United States Penitentiary in Atlanta, Georgia.[302] By January 1937, the District Court of Cleveland had indicted Hunter on "conspiracy" and "postal assault" for the Garrettsville train robbery. Hunter was convicted of these postal charges and sentenced by federal judge Paul Jones at Cleveland to twenty-five years, ten months and nine days. Hunter was transferred to Alcatraz on July 6, 1937.[303]

By April 14, 1943, Freddie Hunter (inmate AZ-402), a forty-three-year-old arthritic and frail at 118 pounds, had joined fellow Alcatraz inmates Floyd Hamilton, James Boarman and Harold Brest in an escape plan. The brazen escape involved conquering the dark and dangerous waters of the San Francisco Bay. The men took two officers hostage while they were working in the industries area. The four men climbed out a window and made their way down to the water's edge. One of the hostages was able to alert the other officers to the escapees. Shots were fired at Boarman, Brest and Hamilton, who were swimming away from the island. Brest was apprehended fairly quickly, and Boarman was hit by gunfire and sank below the water before officers could reach him. Boarman's body was never recovered. Hunter was eventually captured in a cave on the northwest tip of the island by Deputy Warden Ed Miller and FBI agents. Despite hiding under layers of scraps and rubber, it only took a shot from Deputy Miller's .45 automatic, fired into the rock above Hunter's buried head, for Freddie to promptly surrender. Hamilton was originally thought drowned, but after hiding out for two days in a small shoreline cave, Hamilton made his way back up to the industries area, where he was discovered by officers and thrown into isolation.[304]

After putting in his time on Alcatraz, by February 1953 Hunter was out of prison on a conditional release. Due to his severe arthritis, Hunter split his time between northeastern Ohio (reported first address was Leavittsburg, with a second address of Route 1, Diamond in Portage County) and his forty-acre farm, which he purchased for $2,750 just ten miles southwest of Hot Springs. With money saved from his work on the Ohio Turnpike on the outskirts of Youngstown, Hunter was able to purchase his farm and a series of arthritis treatments in Hot Springs.[305]

From June until August 1960, Hunter worked as an oiler for the Harry Miller Excavating Company in Suffield township (located in southern Portage County). Years later, Hunter was recognized by a Trumbull County farmer as one of the gentlemen who had been hunting on his property. As the last surviving Karpis associate, Freddie Hunter died in Hot Springs on November 11, 1982.[306] Karpis's other close associate, Harry Campbell, had died years earlier in Amarillo, Texas, on November 20, 1974.[307]

CHAPTER 18

ALCATRAZ

The Infamous "Pelican" Island

There was never a day you didn't see what the hell you were losing, and what you were missing, you know [Jim Quillen says in the tour audio at Alcatraz]. *It was all there for you to see. There's life. There's everything I want in my life, and it's there. It's a mile or a mile and half away. And yet I can't get to it.*
—*Jim Quillen (AZ-586), 1991 autobiography*

What is the history surrounding America's most notorious federal prison? In November 1932, U.S. Attorney General Homer Cummings received Congressional support to build a maximum-security prison in Alaska. While returning from his Alaskan trip via San Francisco, Cummings's eye caught a sunlit glimpse of the huge brilliant letters reading "U.S. Army Disciplinary Barracks." The letters were like a neon sign on a wall surrounding part of the prison on Alcatraz Island. The attorney general was quick to contact the U.S Army in an effort to "sublease" the prison island and negotiate with the War Department for its use for a period of five years while the Alaska prison was being constructed.[308]

Few prisoners housed at Alcatraz were well-known gangsters like Al Capone. Primarily, those incarcerated there were not prisoners who pulled off bank robberies, kidnapped a business heir or refused to obey the regulations at other federal institutions. Alcatraz inmates were considered and widely reported to be "likely escape risks." Yet Attorney General Cummings claimed that Alcatraz was a place of "confinement" in which "our more dangerous" and "irredeemable" criminals could be sent. "This way," Cummings stated,

View leaving the main cell house on Alcatraz Island, April 2017. *Author's personal collection.*

"[the criminals'] evil influence may not be extended to other prisoners who are disposed to rehabilitate themselves."[309]

While incarcerated, Karpis spent his days and nights with the prison guards he often referred to as "screws" and notoriously dangerous inmates such as Al Capone, George "Machine Gun" Kelly, Arthur "Dock" Barker and Robert Stroud. Former cell house guard George DeVincenzi indicated that Robert Stroud was never in contact with Karpis at Alcatraz. The infamous Stroud was confined for most of his incarceration at Alcatraz in cell 42 in D Block, known as solitary confinement. Recognized as the "Birdman of Alcatraz," Stroud began serving his seventeen-year sentence on the Rock in December 1942. By 1959, because of his failing health, Stroud was transferred to the Medical Center for Federal Prisoners in Springfield, Missouri, where he died in November 1963. Stroud was never incarcerated within the general population at Alcatraz.[310] In 1962, a biographical drama starring Burt Lancaster and directed by John Frankenheimer was released depicting a mostly fictionalized version of Robert Stroud's life.

According to the Bureau of Prisons, the average population of Alcatraz was only about 260 to 275 inmates, with the prison never once reaching its capacity of 336. By the time Alcatraz closed in March 1963, the Rock had accommodated a total of 1,576 prisoners. Many prisoners considered the living conditions of "always one man to a cell" to be better than other federal penitentiaries. Years later, Karpis admitted that he dreamed about Alcatraz during his short-lived confinement at St. Paul and before his transfer to the island in August 1936.[311]

AUGUST 6, 1936:
"THE KISS OFF" (EXILE TO ALCATRAZ)

On August 6, 1936, preparations were being carried out for Karpis's pilgrimage from Leavenworth (just twenty-five miles northwest of Kansas City) to Alcatraz Island. They were all lined up, double file. The inmates were individually handcuffed but shackled by an ankle to the guy beside them. Karpis and nineteen other inmates marched out of the prison building and onto a railroad car awaiting them just inside the confines of the prison walls. Karpis was to make the tenuous two-day and one-night trip to Alcatraz Island, the preeminent federal penitentiary also known as the Big House.

Once boarded on the railway car, Karpis tried his best to peer through the screened and barred windows, where a secured door confined the three feet of train car space at each end. With the slender Karpis pressing his nose against the window, he rose, grinning at a group of curious railroad men.

"How are you?" one of the railroad men asked. The St. Paul felon just lifted his hands, revealing his secured handcuffs. Karpis just smiled broadly and nodded.

A guard then strolled up. "He's here all right," the guard said. "He acts like he's going on a picnic."[312]

Inside his jail on wheels and en route to the West Coast, Karpis and the other convicts made a stop for five minutes in Topeka, Kansas. Situated along the Kansas River, where in the mid-nineteenth century wagon trains made their way west from Missouri, the town where he spent most of his childhood caused Karpis to reminisce.[313]

The former Public Enemy arrived on Alcatraz Island on August 7, 1936, as inmate AZ-325. Unlike Leavenworth, he described Alcatraz as a holding facility with individual stalls and a guard assigned to each prisoner. Alcatraz paled in comparison to the prison population of Leavenworth, a penitentiary that housed more than 1,500 men at one time. Warden James Johnston described Karpis as

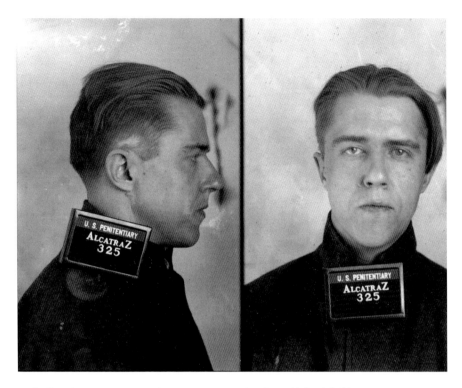

Alvin Karpis's Alcatraz mug shot, August 1936. *San Bruno National Archives.*

a "slight, hardened criminal, who despite repeated fights with other inmates, tried to serve his time as quietly as possible."[314]

Once setting foot on the island, Karpis recalled being less than congenial when first greeted by George "Machine Gun" Kelly. Karpis noted that when he first arrived, Kelly met him out in the recreation yard and warned him about "being too friendly with the common criminals on the island."

Karpis, being the bigshot he believed himself to be, bluntly told Kelly, "Go f--- yourself! I'll talk to whoever I want. There's only one way you spell 'Big Shot' in my dictionary, 'S-H-I-T'!"[315] Needless to say, Kelly remained on the outs with Karpis at Alcatraz. As a matter of fact, former Alcatraz inmate William Radkay (inmate AZ-666) stated in an interview that Kelly told him personally that Karpis had been called out because of his private discussion with the FBI. The FBI agents often conducted private conversations with various inmates to gain vital information. When Karpis returned from one such meeting with the agents, he "didn't say anything" to anyone, Kelly stated in a low and harsh voice.

Right: George "Machine Gun" Kelly, 1933. *Michael Esslinger, Alcatraz historian.*

Below: "Dock" Barker incarcerated at Alcatraz. *Robert Ernst, author of* Robbin' Banks and Killin' Cops.

Kelly called Karpis out: "You god damn little whore." Kelly accused Karpis of being a snitch: "You son of a bitch, you were out there talking to the FBI. You come in here and you ain't saying a god damn thing. Somebody else'll stick their necks out."[316]

"Kelly hated Karpis with a passion just because of the way [Karpis] was always making his booze and not concerned about the food he was screwing up [in the kitchen] for all the other convicts," described former inmate Radkay.[317]

Despite the threats and potential physical danger from other inmates, Karpis never attempted an escape. Yet his former criminal associate "Dock" Barker didn't hesitate to make one. With Ma, Freddie and his two other brothers deceased, it seemed Dock didn't have much to lose. On January 13, 1939, Dock was among five prisoners who tried to escape on a typical foggy night. Placed in the isolation unit (D Block) of Alcatraz for troublesome prisoners, Dock and his fellow inmates sawed through four sets of prison bars with a handsaw while concealing the damage with makeshift putty. After achieving the colossal feat of climbing over the high walls and making an arduous path to the beach, they tried to swim out toward the shore of San Francisco. The tide pushed them back with a vengeance. The escapees were spotted from the guard tower and allegedly warned, but the guards opened fire. Dock was shot in the head and leg, and fellow inmate Dale Stamphill was also shot in the leg, although it was not serious. The three other prisoners were recaptured and sent to solitary confinement. Later that night, Dock succumbed to his wounds. Dale Stamphill later reported that they did not hear any warning from the guards—shots just rang out.[318]

WHAT ARE FOUR WALLS ANYWAY?

Culture shock, depression and anger became a reality for Alvin Karpis once he reached Alcatraz:

I recognize fellows I knew on the outside but they are only pale imitations of their former selves: Machine Gun Kelly, Harry Sawyer, and Dock Barker. Color and life are drained from them all. Looking around again, I pick out "Scarface" Al Capone, much thinner and far more sallow than the last time I saw him. Like the rest, Capone seems to be in a daze. How in the hell could these guys reach this state? This is what Karpis wondered to himself.[319]

One of the cells that became home for Karpis was cell no. 272, and another cell was reported as no. 119B. Alcatraz offered inmates nothing more than highly controlled, monotonous routine. The tedium was designed to indoctrinate the inmate with prison rules and regulations. Karpis witnessed firsthand the truth of the matter: inmates were completely closed off from the world outside.

Most men could extend their arms and touch each wall within their cell. Outside the cell blocks, Broadway was the central corridor that ran through the prison cells. The cells in D Block were segregated and an area where you'd find the isolation cells, where prisoners would be kept in darkness for days on end. The inmates stood by their bunks to be counted every second hour. Every tenth day, razors were issued, and every Wednesday and Saturday there was hot water for a bath. All mail was read by the guards and then retyped on Alcatraz stationery before it was delivered. For two hours a day, residents got to hang around in the walled courtyard while six rifles watched them shuffle back and forth. It's no wonder Alcatraz did strange things to those who tried to leave it.

Alphonse "Al" Capone's mug shot at Alcatraz, August 1934. *San Bruno National Archives.*

Included in part of the inmates' weekly routine were the yard days. Karpis described that on Saturday afternoons and Sunday mornings, the "entire general population [was] loose in the cement area, 'The Yard.'" Karpis had keen memories of this recreation yard, which he characterized as an area of the prison that was "dangerous," sometimes "fatal" and "always unpredictable."[320]

In a 1973 *Rolling Stone* interview, former inmate Charles Earl Johnson (inmate AZ-12), who arrived on the island in 1939, spoke about his own strange experiences—including his close acquaintance with Karpis. Johnson mentioned that Karpis was one of the few "big men" left when he got there in 1939. It was not surprising that Karpis had a corner of the prison yard all to

Al Capone's Alcatraz cell, B Block, cell 181. *Michael Esslinger, Alcatraz historian.*

himself. Johnson got to know Karpis very well as they walked the recreation yard together. He vividly recalled that Karpis spoke about his fears of dying in prison. Johnson also claimed that Karpis admitted he "wanted to die on the streets more than anything else," and "sometimes Karpis would lift his head into the sea breeze and talk about J. Edgar Hoover. Karpis said the name with a spit," recalled Johnson. "That son of a bitch is a coward…a stone coward," Karpis proclaimed.[321]

Johnson also spoke about Al Capone's declining health:

> *"Al Capone's syphilis had more or less fried his brain. He jumped at small noises and dribbled on his chin when he slept. Capone was convinced the cops wanted an excuse to kill him now that he was close to the streets.… He moved slow and his body rose up to his shoulders like two scoops of vanilla," Johnson explained in a somewhat melancholy tone.[322]*

Recalling a happier memory, Charles Earl Johnson said it was rumored that when baseball games were broadcast inside the cell house in the late 1950s, Karpis would "bellow in laughter" when he heard the (William) Hamm Brewery jingle played during the commercial breaks.[323]

THE TROUBLE WITH KARPIS AT ALCATRAZ

During his initial incarceration at Alcatraz, Karpis was known as a prisoner who maintained his privacy. Yet he was known to exhibit many egocentric tendencies and some very confrontational behavior. During his early years, he was described as an inmate who "liked to play the big shot [by] going to the Captain" or other superior and stating, "Captain, I think we can get this thing [inmate strikes] settled." This was the statement made by former prisoner Morton Sobell (AZ-996), who arrived on Alcatraz in 1952. In a January 1980 interview, Sobell claimed that the Bureau of Prisons didn't like any inmate who thought he had any power to settle things, especially inmate strikes. Besides, Alcatraz convicts didn't recognize any leaders. Each inmate believed himself to be a leader in his own right.[324] Sobell's sentiments were confirmed in a report filed by the Bureau of Prisons.

A December 1948 report noted that although Karpis was a "good and a rapid worker, he is considered an evil influence on the other inmates in the kitchen. He is an organizer and agitator, giving instructions to new inmates coming into the kitchen. He is frequently close to the line in getting reported for insolence."[325]

During those first years, Karpis was often held in solitary confinement. This happened on three separate occasions for fist fighting with other prisoners. Karpis's antagonists were later identified as Volney Davis (inmate AZ-271), Allie Anderson (inmate AZ-340) and Albert Bates (inmate AZ-137).[326] On June 8, 1937, during Karpis's second fight, the guard reported that he had to "use force to separate" Karpis and Allie Anderson when the two began fighting in the laundry area. Official documents indicated that Karpis was actually "beaten up by Allie Anderson, inmate #340."

Not four months later, on September 23, 1937, Karpis was again thrown into solitary confinement after participating in a strike. In 1942, he added to his mounting offenses by refusing to work and was yet again segregated. During the single year of 1939, Karpis appeared on three occasions to be inebriated from some form of alcoholic substance. In total, by October 1945, there were eleven reports filed at Alcatraz for Karpis's misconduct.[327]

In his personal view of Karpis, former guard George DeVincenzi (1951–58) characterized the outlaw as a "private individual. [Karpis] worked in the kitchen, and I had to shake him down several times a day. He was a scammer and someone who liked to start trouble and then watch the drama unfold. He'd get everyone else involved and then tip-toe out of it."[328]

DeVincenzi was just twenty-five years old when he began his service on Alcatraz Island as a guard. From the first time he set foot on the island in 1951, DeVincenzi recalled being in contact with Karpis on a regular basis. DeVincenzi was a cell house officer who was stationed at the west end of the penitentiary. This location led into the kitchen where Karpis worked.

DeVincenzi described that Karpis was "looked upon as a leader there [in the kitchen] due to his notoriety as Public Enemy No. 1." Correspondingly, DeVincenzi added that Karpis "was very popular [because] he had a lot of reputation behind him."

According to DeVincenzi, Karpis "was only closely aligned with the kitchen crew. He was the type of inmate who would never talk to you unless he absolutely had to." DeVincenzi made clear that if a guard told Karpis to do something, "he would gladly do it, but he's not the type that would have a cigarette and shoot the breeze with you."[329]

Jim Albright, another young guard serving between 1959 until 1962, also described his impression of Karpis: "Al was the type who was not going to be involved in anything [schemes and so on]. He was the type to say, 'Let me do my time and leave me alone.' He pretty much kept to himself."[330] Of course,

Albright's insight came toward the end of Karpis's time on the island, after the former Public Enemy had become affable toward prison life.

In 1959, Albright was just twenty-four years old and had no prior law enforcement background before he began his service on Alcatraz. As Albright explained, "Karpis was respectful, and a majority of the inmates were. As far as interaction with the inmates, we were told not to give anything to or accept anything from them. We were also informed that you don't let inmates know about your personal life." The last that Albright knew about Karpis was that after he was paroled in 1969 and moved to Canada, he heard that Karpis had "slipped out of Canada and moved to Spain where he hung himself."[331]

As a prisoner who kept to himself, the former outlaw known as "Creepy" was kind of an enigma to some other inmates. Robert Luke (inmate AZ-1118) arrived on the Rock in April 1954 for the conviction of national bank robbery. Luke also attempted an escape from Leavenworth, an offense that primarily contributed to his incarceration at Alcatraz. Taking up residency in the second cell next to Karpis, Luke commented on their remarkable absence of communication. Luke noted that to his recollection, he and Karpis "never spoke or even acknowledged each other" for the entire two years. Luke explained that this was fine with him because he was "more or less a loner."[332] Luke was also well known as a fighter. The likelihood of their situation was that Karpis sized him up and realized there was no way that he could take Luke in a physical altercation, especially given Karpis's gaunt and scrawny build.

Similarly, Robert Schibline (inmate AZ-1355), who arrived on the island in 1958, explained that during his first introduction to Luke, "it was like two Alpha dogs sniffing each other out. Bob was a fighter and I was very good in Martial Arts, so it was like sizing each other up and then walking away with both of us certain that we could take the other and hoping it would never come to that."[333]

As far as avoiding danger, the "hole" (solitary confinement) was one way an inmate could protect himself. Solitary confinement, commonly dubbed the "dark hole," consisted of six cells on the main floor with a barred front view and another solid door outside with just a peephole in it. The main cell house (main corridor) at Alcatraz had no heat. To make matters worse, these cells or "holes" were pitch black. Luke himself described these blocks, consisting of seven-by-seven-foot confinement areas, as void of any material matter whatsoever. These blacked-out holding cells contained only a small cavity in one corner where inmates were told to urinate and defecate. The walls and floor were steel and offered no form of comfort to the naked, cold and shivering prisoner.[334] Ironically, Karpis spent quite a few weeks in this captivity.

In 2018, an interview with the eighty-five-year-old former Alcatraz inmate William "Bill" Baker (inmate AZ-1259) revealed additional insight into "Creepy" Karpis. When asked if Baker knew why folks called Karpis "Creepy," a noticeable staccato laugh followed the question with this response: "First of all, he walked kind of funny, like he was walking on his toes. Physically, if you saw him, he looked a little creepy [or disheveled]."

Baker stated that he wasn't close with Karpis but spoke with him "a couple of times" out in the yard and in the mess hall. Baker remarked that during his "brief conversations" with Karpis, they talked about the ball games and "made a few bets once in a while—small-time bets like a couple of packs of cigarettes." Baker confirmed that Karpis was "pretty well settled down by the late 1950s."

Bill Baker was never a violent criminal, but like so many others, he had a penchant for escaping. Baker was transferred from Leavenworth to Alcatraz in 1957 when he was just twenty-three years old. Baker characterized his time on the Rock in a somewhat soothing response:

> *After the evening meal, we were locked up for the rest of the night. I did a lot of reading and listened to the radio. Before 1959, the radio was like television in that they had all the different programs on such as the soap operas and what not…the sitcoms at night, and they even had the movies on the radio where you'd use your imagination. The* Lone Ranger *was on in the evening and* Amos 'n' Andy. *The radio was not music and news back then.*

In the end, Baker surmised, "If you had a problem [at Alcatraz], you took care of it yourself." But the unexpected lesson that Baker claimed he took away from Alcatraz was that he "learned to do counterfeit payroll checks." And "that's what I did the rest of my life," Baker exclaimed with a bit of braggadocio. This ex-con also stated that he built up his wealth by "stealing a couple cars," claiming that he "loved to do it and made a lot of money." After his release from Alcatraz, Baker didn't get away with these crimes indefinitely. He was in and out of Leavenworth following his release from Alcatraz. Baker claimed, in contrast to official reports and research, that he didn't really know of anyone who had changed their criminal ways after leaving Alcatraz.

"If you're looking for redemption or remorse, you're talking to the wrong guy," Baker spotlighted. "I do not have remorse, nor does any healthy criminal. Anyone [specifically, money criminals] who is healthy psychologically does not have remorse," Baker unapologetically concluded.[335]

As of 2018, Baker remains an overwhelming hit on Alcatraz Island since the release of his 2013 book entitled *Alcatraz #1259*. This book represents the story of a man who never had to hold a job in his life. It is *not* a book about a redeemed William "Bill" Baker who sought to make good of his time on Alcatraz.

Someone who did arrive on the island to do some good was Dr. Milton Daniel Beacher. Stepping onto Alcatraz Island as a young and compassionate doctor on April 26, 1937, the former Rock doc reported in his memoirs that his first day on the job allowed him a close-up glimpse of the notorious Public Enemy, "Creepy" Karpis:

> *A solid door opened and a guard's flashlight played about the form rolled up in the blanket on the floor.*
>
> *Okay, he mumbled. The door was shut. That's Karpis, the guard explained. Somebody smacked him out in the yard. What a shiner!*
>
> *I met Alvin Karpis again the next day when he was taken out of solitary confinement to have a tooth pulled by the visiting dentist. His left eye was black and blue. He was actually [more] nervous about the tooth extraction.*[336]

Likely, this shiner was the result of Karpis's fight with Allie Anderson. Dr. Beacher reported that Karpis was a "hostile and nervous" individual who would fight with other prisoners "at the drop of a handkerchief."[337]

Karpis's difficulties continued at Alcatraz throughout the 1930s and '40s. Those difficulties were intimately witnessed by guard George H. Gregory, who became acquainted with many of the convicts. Arriving on the island in 1947, Gregory—who trained DeVincenzi when he arrived in 1951—said that he recognized Karpis as one of the inmate leaders and self-appointed head of the kitchen crew. Serving as a culinary officer, Gregory got a glimpse of Karpis's persona. During one particular meeting with the kitchen crew, Gregory noticed that Karpis seemed repulsed by the changes to be made by administrators. Gregory recognized Karpis's utter silence and observed his "insolent smile and cold, steely eyes," which signaled to Gregory that Karpis wanted to go on strike.

Gregory understood how powerful Karpis's fearmongering was over the other inmates in the kitchen. "[Karpis] kept everything in line, the work got done. Thus, on the surface, the kitchen had seemed to be running smoothly," recalled Gregory.[338]

One of the kitchen changes that appeared particularly alarming to Karpis and the other inmates required an officer or steward to escort inmates down into the basement. The basement was directly below the kitchen and served as a popular place for a secret rendezvous. According to George Gregory, the inmates had a shower installed down there, and the prisoners had set up a good alarm system so that they knew in advance when an officer was approaching the basement steps. Inmates used the basement in any way they desired. As one would expect, this area served as a haunting environment for consensual and forced sexual behavior. It was solely purposed for inmates to carry out their carnal desires.

The issue of debauchery in the basement led to comments made by former inmate William "Willie" Radkay (inmate AZ-666). Radkay arrived on the island in 1945 for armed robbery and resided in a cell right next to his pal George "Machine Gun" Kelly. Radkay confided in his 2005 memoirs that few were alive who knew how Karpis got the nickname "Creepy."

Radkay suggested, "This just wasn't something you'd openly discuss in public." Radkay reported that he and several of his fellow inmates were at a table in the laundry room waiting for the machines to finish. Radkay recalled that they noticed someone "sneaking around towards the back of the washing machines where all the queers hung out." Radkay went behind the machines to investigate and witnessed Karpis peering at the men back there.

It was claimed that Karpis himself later told Radkay, "He [Karpis] was infatuated with this young queer kid back there and wanted him for himself and would go back there and watch him every chance he got." So, as time went on, Radkay recalled, "When we'd see someone creeping around toward the back of the washers, we'd just remark, 'There goes old Creepy.'"[339]

Author David Ward discovered in a 1981 interview with Radkay that Karpis "implied that he got guys that would go down on him even though he didn't ever do it on anybody else."[340] The takeaway from this, as Ward later emphasized, was that for Alcatraz cons there was a big difference between giving sexual favors and receiving them. Obviously, the inmate always sought to be on the receiving end.

Whether Karpis, not unlike J. Edgar Hoover, strayed into peculiar sexual interludes is arguable, but these taboo acts were common occurrences. Former guard George DeVincenzi witnessed the terror of such a relationship. On his first day at Alcatraz in 1951, DeVincenzi described that he was dressed in "full-pressed uniform" and wearing his "shiny new shoes." The day was just beginning when DeVincenzi witnessed an African American inmate and barber by the name of Freddy Lee Thomas take his barber shears and stab to death his fellow inmate Joseph Barsock. DeVincenzi described a ghastly scene as Thomas stabbed Barsock in the heart, throat and lungs and kept stabbing him. Barsock lay on the floor gasping for air and bleeding to death. Unconsciously mustering a superhuman response, DeVincenzi jumped in, wrangling to separate the two men and ended up with the barber's shears in his hand. As Barsock was stretched out prostrate and dying on the floor, Thomas bent down and audibly voiced, "I love you." Then Thomas kissed Barsock on the face.[341]

Love quarrels and sexual interludes at Alcatraz were an expected and fairly common part of an inmate's life. Former guard Jim Albright declared, "It took on many different forms, including masturbation, sneaking into another inmates' cell for sex, etc."[342] Despite the individual cells and heightened security, the inmates always found ways to make these sexual exchanges happen.

Although Karpis was also faced with the constant threat of unwanted sexual advances, he was able to wield power through his kitchen position. Karpis held a coveted job in the culinary department, for which he showed particular resourcefulness, and served eight years. Three years and eight months were spent as a baker and two years as a cook. Karpis made it incredibly difficult for new inmates to join the kitchen crew without his approval. Former guard George Gregory pointed out that inmates would give up the "coveted position of kitchen worker rather than risk a fight with Karpis and his gang." Those who were part of Karpis's inner circle, or those inmates who were part of the kitchen crew, always ate very well. A few of the head stewards had cooked in some of the best hotels in the world.[343]

Fellow inmate Jim Quillen (AZ-586)—who after a wild crime spree of robbery, kidnapping and escaping San Quentin was sent to Alcatraz in 1942—filled the vacancy in the bakery. Because Quillen had previous kitchen experience at San Quentin, he was given the task and burden of working with Karpis.

CHAPTER 19

BREAD, BOOZE AND BAD BOYS
AT ALCATRAZ

Her soft scent, which has not aroused my nostrils for more than twelve years,
reawakens strange emotions long forgotten.
—*Alvin Karpis, 1951, on working in the kitchen*

Jim Quillen was sure to mention in his 1991 memoirs that Karpis's reputation on the outside did not serve him so well on the inside. Quillen explained that Karpis was not hard to work with, but at times he took himself and his reputation as Public Enemy No. 1 too seriously. "Karpis was not a man given to physical activities and the only altercation I had with him during the two years we worked together came as a result of making happy juice," Quillen amusingly recalled.

During the early 1940s, Quillen and Karpis became partners in making beer that they disguised within stale loaves of bread. Cunningly, they cut the bottoms of the loaves off, hollowed out the centers and then hid small bottles inside. When the bottoms were pushed back into place, the beer could not be detected because these loaves of stale bread were kept in a special section of their bread rack.

Due to someone's negligence, Quillen and Karpis's ruse was discovered and came to an abrupt end. Neither Karpis nor Quillen ever admitted which one failed to bring out enough bread that particular evening to conceal the stale loaves. But on that particular evening, the kitchen guard, Officer Long, went into the bakery and unwittingly pulled a few of the stale loaves from Karpis and Quillen's special rack. When Officer Long picked up the loaves, the bottoms fell off, and their beer stash in the small bottles crashed to the floor. Obviously puzzled, Long examined each loaf on the rack and immediately informed the men of the consequences. If any more beer were found outside the bakery, Long would urinate in the bottles and put them back where he found them. Over the next few months, there remained a serious dry spell in the bakery.[344]

No longer able to turn yeast into alcohol, the strict confines of Pelican Island now only offered Karpis four rights: food, clothing, shelter and medical care. On the upside, Alcatraz was known for having the best food in the federal prison system, as disturbances in prisons were commonly caused by the bad food. A typical meal for dinner included meats, mashed potatoes, gravy, vegetables, bread, dessert and coffee. Inmates were permitted to eat as much as they wanted within twenty minutes as long as they wasted no food. If they wasted any food, typically any privileges would be revoked.[345]

Musical instruments were later added to a list of privileges. Al Capone became so cooperative with the Alcatraz strict modes of discipline that he racked up enough time for "good behavior" and was permitted to play the banjo in the Alcatraz prison band. This band was known as the Rock Islanders, and it performed Sunday concerts for the other inmates. Capone also played the mandola (resembles a large mandolin). In fact, the former mob boss boasted that he could play more than five hundred songs. Capone even wrote a love song he entitled "Madonna Mia," which was published posthumously in 2009.[346]

With this new privilege, Karpis took up the guitar, an instrument that would years later lead to an introduction with a diabolical Californian named Charlie Manson. After being transferred from Alcatraz to McNeil Island in April 1962, Karpis met the young Manson. Karpis wrote about this country's most notorious cult leader in his second autobiography:

> *This kid approaches me to request music lessons. He wants to learn guitar and become a music star. "Little Charlie" is so lazy and shiftless, I doubt if he'll put in the time required to learn. The youngster has been in institutions all of his life—first orphanages, then reformatories, and finally federal prison. His mother, a prostitute, was never around to look after him. I decide it's time someone did something for him, and to my surprise, he learns quickly. He has a pleasant voice and a pleasing personality, although he's unusually meek and mild for a convict. He never has a harsh word to say and is never involved in even an argument.*

After Manson became fairly proficient on the guitar, he asked Karpis for help in acquiring some playing gigs in Las Vegas. Manson was well aware of Karpis's kinship with nightclub and casino owners there. Luckily, Karpis passed on Manson's offer, leaving Manson to his own devices when it came to his music career.[347]

LAST DAYS OF ALCATRAZ

Once prison officials felt that a man no longer posed a threat and could follow the rules (an average of five years on Alcatraz), he could be transferred back to another federal prison to finish his sentence and be released.[348] Despite Karpis's slow but positive adjustment to prison life, he far exceeded the five years at Alcatraz and the average age of thirty for its prisoners. This was thanks, in part, to J. Edgar Hoover.

Without mincing words, the Bureau director opposed Karpis's release and stated in 1962, "In view of the ruthless crimes perpetrated by Karpis, I wanted to let you know of the alleged efforts to get him released from prison. By reason of his notorious background, Karpis is certainly not entitled to any consideration."[349]

In his efforts to prevent Karpis's release, Hoover sent a copy of this letter to James Bennett, director of the Bureau of Prisons. In addition to the letter, Hoover demanded that the FBI be informed of any efforts made to transfer or release Karpis in the future. "God forbid this tyrant be allowed to walk the streets," Hoover proclaimed.[350] By November 1961, Karpis was set to be transferred back to Leavenworth, but after the Bureau's field office in San Francisco was notified, those plans were quickly scrapped.

Karpis was eligible for parole after fifteen years, and his original parole date was scheduled for July 26, 1951. Karpis's eligibility for parole came and went, as the former outlaw declined to file an application. By 1955, Karpis still maintained that he did not wish to file for parole, often citing that he would never receive it.[351]

Hoover wasn't Karpis's only hang-up in gaining parole. The detainer against Karpis for the murder of Sheriff C.R. "Roy" Kelly in West Plains, Missouri, was still outstanding. Anticipating Karpis's parole, the sheriff's widow, Lulu Kelly Oliver, filed a complaint in a felony case against Karpis for her husband's murder. The complaint filed by Lulu Kelly was followed with a detainer from the current sheriff Lester Davis.[352] It wasn't until

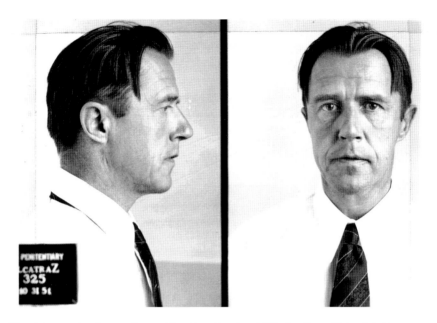

Karpis's mug shot for parole consideration, October 1951. *San Bruno National Archives.*

October 7, 1952, that this murder charge was withdrawn. Due to lack of force by the sheriff's widow and the lack of evidence to pursue the case, the detainer was terminated.[353]

Karpis remained at Alcatraz until April 1962, leaving less than one year before the prison closed on March 21, 1963.[354] The year 1962 was also the same year when Karpis's fellow inmate Robert "Bob" Schibline (AZ-1355), a convicted bank robber, was released. During an interview with Schibline, he recalled Karpis as a difficult inmate during his early incarceration at Alcatraz, which Karpis later admitted. But Karpis mellowed during his later years, claimed Schibline:

> *He was keeping his nose clean and trying to get out. As far as J. Edgar Hoover is concerned, Karpis swears that he held no animosity towards Hoover. Although, as Karpis was saying this, he said it in a way that I knew he was not telling the truth. I, myself, never liked Hoover and told Karpis so, but I never really hated him. After I got out of prison and in May of 1972 when Hoover died, I went to the corner tavern that I did my drinking in and talked to the owner about renting it for the following Saturday to have a celebration of [Hoover's] death. That Saturday cost*

me almost $800, but it was the best time I had in a very long while. Today, I don't throw parties anymore when someone I don't like dies (like an Alcatraz guard), but when I hear of one kicking off, I always have a few shots of good Cognac to the day!

So most of our talks were about fingerprints, and it was the main reason for me walking the yard with Karpis. I wanted to pick his brain about fingerprint removal, his lack of fingerprints, and he seemed very interested in my plan to [transplant] *my prints, not remove them. He said that his doc used acid, numbed the fingertips, and then pared down the skin with a scalpel.* [Karpis said] *not to try this way as it was very painful. I assumed he was talking about Dr. Moran, but Karpis just called him his "quack."* My [transplant idea was a process where] *the skin is cut around the first joint and around the fingernail and then removed at a thickness of 1 or 2 mm. The thumb would go on the big toe, and each finger in turn would go onto the next toe until each finger was now your toe print. After a few months, the scar would disappear in the crease of the joint, and you'd be left with some new identification…you would be a new person with no record if ever fingerprinted. Karpis seemed impressed with the idea.*[355]

Believe it or not, the first time I met Karpis was before I ever got to Alcatraz. He and I were on the same chain when I went to the Rock in 1958. We had a warden at Leavenworth that did not like Alcatraz inmates and framed Alvin on a phony charge, shipping him back [to Alcatraz in October 1958 after only seven months back at Leavenworth]. [Oddly enough, Karpis] *did say that he was married once, but I never heard about a son.*[356]

Schibline went on to describe what he believed to be his worst recollection of doing time on the Rock. Without hesitation, Schibline recalled, "That's easy for me…it was the fact you were locked up all the time. It has affected me to this day! After being free and out of prison for over 50 years, I have never locked my house door with me in it! Never! To tell the truth, I don't even know if it works?"[357]

During his efforts to be transferred, Karpis cited persecution by both the FBI and the various wardens. It was only when former Alcatraz guard Paul Madigan became warden that circumstances began to change for Karpis. In 1955, Paul Madigan, or "Promising Paul," as his guard staff called him (he made promises he never kept), had replaced Edwin B. Swope as warden.[358] Madigan has been cited as the only warden to work his way up through the prison staff hierarchy, having begun his career as a correctional officer during the 1930s. On May 21, 1941, Madigan reportedly played a key role in "squashing" an escape attempt after being held hostage. This heroism led to a promotion to associate warden for Madigan, and the rest is history.[359]

When Paul Madigan became warden at Alcatraz in 1955, the prison underwent a modernization. Radio headsets were installed, and the parole committee began to work on the "old-timers'" cases. In 1958, Warden Madigan put together a proposal to parole Karpis. It was accepted, and Karpis was sent to Leavenworth with a plan to serve out his final year in February 1958. Serving out his remaining sentence at Leavenworth would also allow Karpis to be closer to his family.[360] Unfortunately, circumstances didn't go as Madigan planned and as Karpis desperately hoped.

It was Frank Loveland, assistant director of the Bureau of Prisons, who received an "urgent request" on September 19, 1958, from Warden Chester Looney at Leavenworth. In his message, Looney reported that he suspected Karpis was instigating complaints about the food and that Karpis was a bad influence on the other inmates.

Karpis was described by warden Looney as someone who had "always been able to control other inmates and cause them to create problems while he [Karpis] drops into the background." Looney identified Karpis as a serious threat because the warden claimed that the former outlaw had "an unusual interest in an escape plot that was uncovered [there]."[361] Two days later, and after only seven months in Leavenworth, Karpis was on his way back to Alcatraz and again under the supervision of Warden Paul Madigan.

Despite the unpleasantries with the warden at Leavenworth, Karpis declared that he had a friend in Warden Madigan. So when Madigan was transferred to McNeil Penitentiary in Washington State, Karpis thought he was doomed on Alcatraz. No other warden at any other institution would accept Karpis. Coupled with being recognized as an inmate who would stir up trouble, Karpis was known by prison staff to be rather nervous and prone to symptoms of stress. Specifically, the aging former outlaw had arthritis of the spine and deep-vein thrombosis. By late 1961, Karpis had experienced several back injuries and was in and out of the hospital. To add insult to injury, his anxieties over another transfer were causing him prolonged and severe stomach issues. Karpis was at the end of his rope, pondering the likelihood that he would die at Alcatraz.[362]

But hope was a mainstay. Karpis claimed that Warden Madigan told the director of the Federal Bureau of Prisons, James Bennett, that he would "personally" be responsible for Karpis at McNeil Island. "I'll take the rap for anything he does wrong," Madigan confidently proclaimed.

If Karpis was to be transferred with him to McNeil Penitentiary, Madigan guaranteed Karpis's good behavior.[363] After some forceful persuasion, Madigan secured a final parole opportunity for Karpis on McNeil Island.[364] On Friday, April 6, 1962, Karpis was making his final goodbyes to his friends out on the recreation yard. In Karpis's own words, he described what would later become reminiscent of a Hollywood scene starring Clint Eastwood in the title role of escapee Frank Morris:

> *The Anglin brothers are working themselves into good physical condition on the handball court; they hang in the background nodding as I leave the yard but show enough courtesy not to be seen with me by the ever watchful guards. I'm relieved to be out of Alcatraz before they make their play. If the plaster of paris is ever connected with me, it will be the end of my transfer…but there are obligations a convict has to himself and to escape which no one who has never been locked in a cage can hope to appreciate.*[365]

Because he worked in the hospital at the time, it was Karpis who secured the plaster of Paris for the Anglin brothers. This composite material, or papier-mâché, was utilized so that the Anglin brothers and Frank Morris could construct dummies to act as decoys. Throughout its years of operation as a federal prison, there were fourteen known attempts to escape from Alcatraz, involving thirty-six inmates. The Bureau of Prisons reported that of these would-be escapees, twenty-three were captured, six were shot and killed during their attempted getaways, two drowned and five went missing and were presumed drowned.[366] The three of the five of these who "went missing" were John and Clarence Anglin and Frank Morris.

On Saturday, April 7, 1962, the boat carrying Karpis crossed the turbulent and shark-infested waters of the San Francisco Bay. It would be McNeil Island Penitentiary where Karpis himself admitted that reform was awaiting him, due largely to his friend Warden Madigan.[367]

Not long after Karpis's departure, Attorney General Robert Kennedy closed the federal prison on March 21, 1963. Kennedy cited its high cost per prisoner and its emphasis on retribution rather than rehabilitation. Today, the former federal penitentiary serves as a public museum maintained by the National Park Service and is visited by more than 1.7 million people each year.

Chapter 20

A CHANGED MAN
AFTER ALCATRAZ

I have nothing but contempt for J. Edgar Hoover. For the rest, there are no apologies, no regrets, no sorrows, and no animosity. What happened happened.
—*Alvin Karpis,* The Alvin Karpis Story

By April 1965, Karpis's adjustment on the Washington island had been reported as "excellent." Many prison officials expressed their admiration for Karpis's favorable attitude toward the institution. Consequently, Warden Ray Meier (1966–70), who succeeded Paul Madigan at McNeil, endorsed Karpis's parole for deportation. For Karpis and many other prisoners, McNeil Federal Penitentiary represented a successful rehabilitative program. In less than three years, Karpis graduated from a ten-man cell and close custody to the Summit House and minimum custody. Karpis became one of the strongest boosters at the institution and was selected as a member of the Summit House Steering Committee. All those who came into contact with Karpis witnessed that he was living proof of a responsible individual who would make good on the outside.[368]

It was Frank Roberts Jr., executive director of the Catholic Rehabilitation Service in Montreal, who aided and counseled Karpis while incarcerated at McNeil Island. This agency served as the official parole sponsor for the Canadian government. Since Karpis's original inquiry to the agency back in September 1960 (while still at Alcatraz), Mr. Roberts had worked as a liaison between Karpis and the parole board. In a formal letter, Roberts happily assumed supervision of Karpis upon his release on parole. Additionally, Roberts offered Karpis

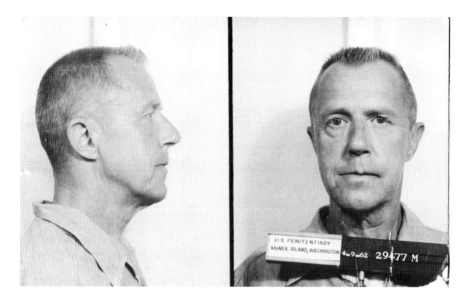

Karpis's McNeil Island mug shot, April 9, 1962. *San Bruno National Archives.*

hospitality in his own home in Montreal and a welcomed "accommodation in [his] own family." Roberts also promised Karpis employment for a period of twelve to eighteen months as an accountant for a Montreal company.[369]

By 1968, Karpis appeared a changed man. In fact, a letter written by Robert "Bob" Anderson, a businessman from Seattle, Washington, described how he was "measurably impressed" by Karpis. In Anderson's written estimation, Karpis had provided "effective counseling efforts with several young men" who came to his AA group at Karpis's insistence. Because of Karpis's positive influence, those young adults had shaped into "serious, sensibly-motivated men," Anderson confidently stated.[370]

RELEASE AND REDEMPTION

It was November 27, 1968, and nearly thirty-three years after Karpis's arrest, when the officials with the Department of Justice finally announced that he would be released on parole for "deportation only." Effective January 14, 1969, Alvin Karpis, at the time in his twilight years at sixty years of age, was turned over to Canadian immigration and transported to Montreal, Canada, where he quietly planned to live out his days.[371]

Photo depicting Karpis with James Carty, his attorney, at a press conference shortly after his release from McNeil Federal Penitentiary, January 14, 1969. *From The Cleveland Press Collection, Michael Schwartz Library, Cleveland State University.*

Karpis arriving at the Montreal International Airport from Vancouver on January 15, 1969. *From The Cleveland Press Collection, Michael Schwartz Library, Cleveland State University.*

Despite the consensus that his fingerprints remained intact, Karpis had some difficulty obtaining a Canadian passport. In fact, former FBI agent Thomas McDade recalled when he visited Karpis in Spain in 1978 that the tips of Karpis's fingers "were completely smooth, not a sign of a ridge." Karpis told McDade that when he went to retrieve a resident permit in Spain, the female clerk tried five or six times to get Karpis's print. Finally, she gave up and let him go.[372]

By 1971 and during his first tour across Canada for his autobiography entitled *Public Enemy Number One*, Karpis presented himself more as a business professional rather than as a terrifying 1930s gangster. Karpis also added a bit of humor along the way. Robert Livesey, the coauthor of Karpis's second book, *On the Rock*, revealed him to be "a former outlaw showing no signs of his criminal background to those who met him." Livesey further characterized Karpis as a "friendly, gregarious grandfather figure who charmed and pleased almost anyone he met. He was also constantly in relationships with women 20 years younger than he was, in his sixties"[373]

Karpis in a Canada grocery store, undated. *Michael Esslinger, Alcatraz historian.*

Former Canadian CKCK radio broadcaster and open-line commentator Lorne Harasen interviewed Karpis twice during the ex-gangster's Canadian tour. For the radio interview, Harasen stated that Karpis arrived at the studio in a "suit and tie that had seen better days. He was stooped over a bit and he was courteous and not overly loud of voice." Harasen remarked that Karpis "looked more like your 'Uncle Mike' rather than a glamorous crook." The radio broadcaster concluded that "Old Creepy" was "meek and placid," and the only time that Karpis's countenance became "stormy" was when he was asked about his son or when J. Edgar Hoover's name was mentioned.

According to Harasen, Karpis's biggest challenge was adjusting to life outside of prison. Life had changed drastically from the time Karpis was first incarcerated at Alcatraz in 1936 to when he was paroled in 1969. After his release, one of the places that Karpis was most curious about was the supermarket. While visiting his local grocery store in Canada, Karpis was baffled by the change from the corner grocery store that he had frequented as a boy. By the end of Harasen's radio interview with Karpis, the described "contrite and meek" Karpis had admitted that his life of crime was a "wasted life."[374]

CHAPTER 21

DEVOTED DELANEY

Honey, I don't want you to worry about Raymond
as he will be well taken care of as long as you are in there.
—*letter from Karpis to Delaney dated June 13, 1936, written from St. Paul jail*

Dolores Delaney gave birth to Karpis's son, Raymond, in February 1935, and the child was turned over to the care of Karpis's parents in Chicago. His nephew, Albert Grooms, claimed that both Karpis and Delaney agreed (after the Atlantic City shootout) to name their son Raymond. Grooms stated that the name Raymond seemed appropriate to Karpis, given that it was one of his aliases. Karpis often took the names Raymond Hadley and Ray Miller.[375]

For Delaney, harboring a fugitive only required her to serve a maximum of two years per count. It appeared that J. Edgar Hoover was responsible for "strongly suggesting" that Delaney receive three sentences for harboring Karpis. Consequently, this prevented her from having contact with her son throughout his early childhood. Delaney had three sentences that required that the two sentences run consecutively and the third case running concurrently. Delaney and Wynona Burdette entered Milan Federal Correctional Institution in Michigan on March 29, 1935.[376]

As Karpis's moll, Delaney had done some talking with the feds. She gave some names, dates and places but never implicated Karpis for any of his crimes. Delaney gave a signed statement to Bureau agents while she was contained at the Ramsey County Jail in St. Paul. She was only twenty years old and likely well aware of the consequences of her testimony.

Despite her incarceration and separation from her son, Delaney spoke with hope about Mr. and Mrs. Karpowicz bringing "Little Ray" to see her. The young Dolores described him with such joy: "His eyes are so big and blue and his hair is real light—what little there is of it. He looked just like a big doll. He's doing his best to talk, too, and he says, 'mama' just as big as you can. Gee, do you think by any chance he knew I was his Mother?"[377]

One can only imagine the suffering that Delaney endured while imprisoned and unable to see and eventually raise her son and only child. In her letter to Mr. and Mrs. Karpowicz dated December 10, 1935, Delaney wrote, "Give my great big son a bushel of hugs and kisses from me. It's hard to believe that he is almost a year old….Tell him his Mother thinks of him all the time and wants him to grow up to be a good boy so you will be proud of him. Is he trying to talk yet? I'd sure love to hear him."[378]

Initially delayed, the writing privileges between Karpis and Delaney were granted by the Bureau of Prisons. Karpis had anxiously written to Delaney inquiring about her adjustment to prison life and about their son. Despite their apparent affection for each other and their son, Raymond, the star-crossed lovers never reconnected in person.

After years of captivity, Delaney was granted a "conditional release" from Milan on November 30, 1938. She was under the guidance and tracking of a probation officer until 1940.[379] Although dedicated to begin a new life, Delaney never saw her son again after those few short visits in prison. Albert Grooms claimed that young Raymond came to visit him over the years. During the visits, Raymond asked Grooms what his mother's married name was, but Grooms told Raymond that he didn't know. Grooms did state that he knew Dolores was living somewhere around St. Paul after her parole in 1940.[380]

As an adult, Raymond eventually recognized Dolores Delaney as his mother but had adopted his paternal grandparents as his parents.[381] Raymond never visited his mother as an adult, and the exact circumstances surrounding the reasons for this permanent estrangement remain unknown. Throughout his life, it appeared that Raymond had no knowledge of the whereabouts of his mother, but Dolores did correspond a few times with Mr. and Mrs. Karpowicz for several years following Raymond's birth in 1935. Sometime in 1937, Dolores sent a postcard to the Karpowicz household—this was her last contact. Although Raymond had never met his father before the visit to Leavenworth in 1958, he did correspond often by letter while his father was at Alcatraz.[382] In his visit to see his father in late March 1958, the tall and thin twenty-three-year-old Raymond indicated that his father felt he would not be

Dolores Delaney (later known as Dee Higby) pictured with her husband, Clifford Higby, in New Orleans during December 1940. *Susan Henry (step-granddaughter).*

granted a parole. Regrettably, Raymond also noted that he had never seen his mother.[383]

Dolores did eventually remarry. The gentleman's name was Clifford Higby, and he was a righteous and upstanding citizen. Higby was a former policeman and burgeoning musician from Chicago. According to Dolores's step-granddaughter, Susan Henry, Dolores had met Clifford (Henry's maternal grandfather) at a club in Chicago where he was performing in a band. Susan Henry, who was born in 1944, presumed that Clifford and Dee (Dolores) were married sometime before her birth.

Dee was a very "prim and proper" young lady, stated Ms. Henry. "She and my grandfather were the typical grandparents. They had a very good relationship, and I enjoyed spending a lot of time with them," she fondly reminisced. Ms. Henry described her step-grandmother as "very small statured and quiet," and yet she distinguished Dee as a sort of "prima donna." As a young girl, Ms. Henry recalled that she often found a need to be "perfect" in the presence of her step-grandmother.

To Ms. Henry's amazement, Dee never once spoke of her checkered past—not even a passing mention that she had a son named Raymond. According to Ms. Henry, Dee claimed that she could never physically have children with Clifford, and so no children were conceived during the marriage. Dee remained close-lipped about her personal history and never once discussed her sisters, mother or even her father. Ms. Henry explained that Dee only mentioned she attended Catholic school as a young girl and that she "loved her brother, Bud—whom Dee only mentioned one time."[384]

Dee's long-lost son, Raymond, married a lady named Nancy, whose parents owned a grocery store on Foster Avenue in Chicago. Eventually, they had a son. Unfortunately, Raymond Alvin Karpowicz inherited a life of crime and passed away in October 2001 in Chicago. Sadly, Raymond and Nancy's son, Damon, preceded his parents in death, as the boy

Dolores Delaney (Dee Higby) with her husband, Clifford, July 3, 1939. *Susan Henry (step-granddaughter).*

passed away suddenly at age fifteen in 1988.[385] Nancy remarried, but understandably, she never wished to speak to anyone about her past life with the younger Ray Karpis.

Without any public pageantry, Dolores died in Mesa, Arizona, on April 24, 1985, at the age of sixty-nine. Her modest obituary indicated that Dolores, at the time of her death, was known as Dee M. Higby. The announcement also indicated that Dee was born in South Dakota and moved to Arizona from Indiana around 1970. Dee was survived by her granddaughter, Susan Henry, and her sister, Helen Wilson (formerly known as Helen "Babe" Riley).[386] The family maintains that after Dolores's probation in 1940, she met and married their maternal grandfather, Clifford. By all appearances, this onetime Karpis moll—formerly known as Dolores Delaney—led a normal and seemingly uneventful life.

CHAPTER 22

HOLLYWOOD CAME CALLING

W e are going towards production," reported Harold Hecht in a letter to Karpis dated October 27, 1976. Hecht, a producer for the highly anticipated production of a John Frankenheimer film entitled *The Last Public Enemy*, had been in close correspondence with Karpis. The men were putting together a screenplay by the great Michael Mann and based on the autobiography of Karpis's scandalous life.[387]

As previously mentioned, former FBI special agent Thomas McDade met the former gangster in Spain during the late 1970s. McDade had written the only known diary of a Depression-era FBI agent. As a long-retired lawman, McDade stated that he became fascinated with Karpis after reading his autobiography and decided to write Karpis a "brief note." Not expecting a response, after several months had passed, McDade was pleased when he received a long letter from Karpis. McDade expressed that he was surprised by the "vitality" of Karpis's writing. Karpis's letter "exuded energy, intelligence, enterprise and imagination," remarked McDade. The former Public Enemy welcomed the correspondence, and so an international exchange of letters began between the two men.

As the two men's written communication progressed, they finally agreed to meet. It was a trip with friends that allowed McDade to meet up with Karpis in Spain in the spring of 1978. McDade admitted that he was a little uneasy.

Upon their first introduction, McDade described Karpis, whom he called Al, as "slender and well dressed in a dark suit." Once shaking the hand of his former adversary, McDade commented that Al's "pale blue eyes and crew cut made him look younger than I knew him to be."

Former FBI special agent Thomas McDade (*left*) and Alvin Karpis (*right*) in Spain in 1978. *Jared McDade, son of Special Agent Thomas McDade.*

After only a few minutes of small talk, Al was willing to divulge some of his account of the Edward George Bremer kidnapping. McDade recalled Karpis's honesty: "Oh, that fellow Bremer, how tired I got of him. I guarded him at the hideout for three weeks and all he did was complain about the food."[388]

When McDade questioned Karpis about the other members of the gang, Karpis asserted that he was closest to Freddie Barker and that Ma was a sort of "surrogate mother" to him. McDade insisted that he never mentioned his own involvement in the fatal Barker shooting on Lake Weir. No one was ever certain whether Karpis knew that McDade was present at the shootout scene, including McDade himself.

As a former FBI agent, McDade was working to arrange the film of Karpis's life with director John Frankenheimer. The movie that Paramount Pictures was to film was never launched. This artistic creation, which was to recast Karpis as a new folk hero, never saw the lights dim in the theaters. Originally, the script was written to portray Karpis as the last important Public Enemy in American history. Harold Hecht had written to Karpis that the film would help Karpis "come off very well in it."[389]

The Karpis film was to mark the second consecutive movie for Paramount Pictures and Frankenheimer. This film was also set to reunite Frankenheimer with producer Harold Hecht. The two men previously worked together on *Birdman of Alcatraz* and *The Young Savages*. The movie was slated to roll in December 1976, but sadly the production never was completed due in part to Karpis's untimely death in 1979.[390] To this day, the actor who was to play Karpis remains a mystery.

In 1985, on the fiftieth anniversary of the Barker shooting, former agent Thomas McDade revisited the Barker cottage, and the bullet holes were still eerily visible throughout the house. In the fall of 2012, the house was put on the market for $1 million.[391]

CHAPTER 23

END OF AN OUTLAW ERA

I always wanted to be the outlaw. And that's to a certain extent how I've lived.
—*James Frey, journalist, author and screenwriter born in Cleveland, Ohio*

From 1933 until Karpis's capture in 1936, the FBI had contributed to the conviction of 11,153 people for violations of federal laws. This included 152 bank robbers and more than 330 kidnappers and extortionists. It was estimated by statisticians that during the 1930s for every $1 spent in FBI operations, $7 were "returned to the taxpayers." In 1935, there were forty convictions under the federal kidnapping law, and $150,000 in ransom money was recovered.[392] However, only about $100,000 of the ransom money that was recovered by the FBI was that of the Karpis-Barker Gang. As documented by FBI reports, 1935 witnessed the nation's law enforcement officers killing nearly four hundred members of the underworld.[393]

By the time of Hoover's death in May 1972, criticism of his autocratic power over the lives and liberties of his fellow Americans hadn't let up. Despite his lifelong stack of accolades, the decade that began in 1970 brought the FBI director the most sustained and devastating crossfire of his entire career. Undoubtedly, Hoover left behind a legacy characterized by two extremes. For better or worse, he built the FBI into a modern, national organization stressing the highest level of professionalism and scientific crime-fighting techniques. Hoover's unchallengeable position as director of the FBI was hardly hurt by the fact that he was also the keeper of the files—otherwise known as the mountain of personal dossiers the

Karpis discussing his upcoming parole, 1968. Photo taken at McNeil Island Federal Penitentiary. *Michael Esslinger, Alcatraz historian.*

FBI had put together. Hoover's collection of documents consisted mostly of unproven allegations during Hoover's long decades of snooping. Unfortunately, no diaries or intimate letters of Hoover's have survived. Hoover's private files, also containing private letters and sensitive office documents, were destroyed immediately following his death and upon his orders as dictated to his lifelong secretary, Helen Gandy.

When all was said and done, Alvin "Creepy" Karpis outlasted J. Edgar Hoover in mortality though not in legacy—despite Karpis's record-setting twenty-five years on the infamous prison island. The former Public Enemy, in the ten years preceding his arrest in 1936, compiled a record of fifty-four aliases, fifteen bank robberies, fourteen murders, three jail breaks and two high-profile kidnappings. He moved from Montreal, Canada, to Torremolinos, Spain, in 1973. The capture of Karpis essentially ended the age of the big-name Depression-era criminals and sent Karpis to an almost timeless tenure on the Rock. The former Public Enemy took his place in history among the top ten unflinching badasses to ever set foot on Alcatraz Island.

Karpis's nephew, Albert Grooms, stated that his uncle told him at least once after his release from prison that "he'd go down a different path on life's highway if he could live his life over again." And yet, Karpis also indicated that the banks should have been accountable. "Alvin was bitter about that," claimed Grooms.[394] Albin Francis Karpowicz died in Torremolinos, Spain, on August 26, 1979, at the age of seventy-one. Throughout the decades, the death of Karpis has been described as a suicide due to a purported overdose of alcohol and pills.[395] According to

J. Edgar Hoover in 1970. *Author's personal collection.*

Robert Livesey, this story is false. Even today, Livesey rightly continues to describe Karpis as "not the type of person to give up and take his own life. [Karpis] was awaiting the publication of the book that I wrote with him, *On the Rock*, but most importantly, he was a survivor; he had survived 33 depressing years in prison." This statement by Livesey was confirmed by a retraction in the *Chicago Sun-Times*. Police declared that Karpis died of "natural causes [heart attack]…contradicting earlier reports."[396] Karpis was originally buried at the San Miguel Cemetery in Spain and laid to rest in plot no. 2300 in 1979. On May 28, 1999, when his "permanency" was expired and no one claimed his remains, he was reburied in a communal mass grave. Today, it remains nearly impossible to find any palpable remnant of Karpis's physical existence.

FINAL THOUGHTS

The Legacy

The national implications of this last great train robbery in American history are difficult to turn away from as related in this work. Karpis was the last Public Enemy of the Depression era and J. Edgar Hoover's first arrest, a markedly important event that secured Hoover's prolonged tenure as FBI director. Moreover, Karpis successfully pulled off the train heist by becoming the first outlaw to escape a crime by airplane. The Garrettsville Train Depot, located in northeastern Ohio, played a critical role in Karpis's capture by Hoover and his select group of special agents known as Government Men (G-Men).

It is important to remember that despite the pressured hunt for Karpis in Ohio at the time, Karpis decidedly chose this train depot as the location for his unintended last crime. This natural setting situated on the Erie Railroad's Cleveland–Youngstown line put it in direct contact with the steel mill payrolls. As Karpis concluded, this was not an impromptu robbery:

> *The job was guaranteed to be a big extravaganza. It carried cash enough to cover the weekly salaries of workers in all the giant mills of Youngstown. I organized the job down to the last move. I cased the trains, ran the escape roads, plotted the getaway with as much thoroughness as I'd brought to any job.... Garrettsville had the advantage of its short distance from Port Clinton.*[397]

Throughout the decades, this local event has been adopted as the backstory for the mascot of the James A. Garfield School District's

A James A. Garfield High School cheerleader being greeted by the G-Man mascot, 1991. *Jaguar Yearbook staff.*

athletic teams in Garrettsville, Ohio—the author's alma mater. As referenced by Dr. James Pesicek, a lifelong resident of Garrettsville, he had always understood that the "fighting G-Men" mascot represented the Government Men who flooded the area after the train robbery. Characterized by an inspector with a magnifying glass, trench coat and the Sherlock Holmes deerstalker-style cap, this mascot is the only one of its kind in the United States. Likewise, the Garfield G-Men mascot is widely included among the lists of the most distinctive and unusual high school mascots in the country.

Rather than just focusing on Karpis's physicality as a kidnapper and bank pilferer, this true crime story illustrates how this last Public Enemy did not live in a gangster's paradise. In contrast, at his height of public notoriety, Americans considered J. Edgar Hoover the hero. He made the G-Man brand so popular that it was harder to become an FBI agent than to be accepted into an Ivy League college. Hoover and his G-Men achieved powerful influence for the FBI and defined this federal agency as the protector of national security for our country's future. Despite Hoover's towering reputation, the top G-Man was not without reproach. Hoover was an egomaniac who became tyrannical, ruling the FBI as his personal kingdom while habitually abusing power.

As far as Hoover's influence on the legacy of Alvin "Creepy" Karpis, during the thirty-three years that Karpis spent in federal prison, Karpis bemoaned that it "grated on [him] that Americans" had been deceived into celebrating Hoover as one of the greatest lawmen in American history. Of course, this celebration of Hoover was heavily aligned with Hoover's account of Karpis's arrest.[398] What happened to Karpis likely happened as he reported. For the rest of the story, Karpis today would say that you'd have to ask J. Edgar Hoover.

Since the 1930s, many of these battle sites from the War on Crime remain as they did then—out-of-the-way spots, now dusty and cobwebbed, of interest only to history buffs. Gone but not forgotten, this depot site in Garrettsville remains a country road. In a meadow of thick grass and tall hemlocks, the meandering trails dominate this right-of-way between Mantua and Garrettsville.

Today, this now desolate former location of the Cleveland railway, winding its way through the edge of the Garrettsville town limits, serves only to sustain the quaint historic settlement that originally grew up around the town's gristmill and maple syrup center.[399] Since Karpis's caper, not one individual has heard the echoes of machine gun fire or ghostly screams of terrified victims. There's no reminder of Alvin "Creepy" Karpis's Wild West venture other than the commemorative historical marker that proudly displays "'Creepy' Karpis and The Last Great Train Heist."

Still living in a charming and rural part of northeastern Ohio, among the cluster of close-knit neighbors, I settle on this story to tell those "out of towners" when they ask whether anything exciting ever happens in this neck of the woods. "This is a real crime story, taking place in my hometown," I say with a bit of smug satisfaction. To this stealthy thief known as "Creepy" Karpis, Garrettsville proved to be an easy score. Regardless of the many decades that have passed, people here and everywhere remain very interested in the lore of gangsters, drawn to the idea of that era.

Undoubtedly, this last great train heist helped to pave a path for Karpis to Alcatraz and prevented the spectacular fall of J. Edgar Hoover and his coveted FBI. Despite the fact that Karpis still remains fairly unexplored when compared to his fellow celebrity prisoners at Alcatraz, visitors can still view Karpis's mug shot as a main attraction on the wall of the abominable cell house. And many decades after Alcatraz closed its doors and headed into retirement, the former super-max facility still conjures up images of an inescapable prison where the world-class badasses atoned for their crimes.

In the end, can we trust the words of an admitted thief? Can Karpis's words stack up against the official records of the FBI and the testimony of J. Edgar Hoover? There is no final jeopardy here. What has been stated with certainty is that Bill Trent, Karpis's first coauthor, never once in all his fact checking found a Karpis story to be in error.

Karpis's story reminds us all of what J. Edgar Hoover himself emphasized: "What's important at this time is to re-clarify the difference between hero and villain." In the reading of this story, an individual is intrigued to ask, "Who was the *real* villain and who was the hero?" The answer? There are stories where the villain becomes the hero, but this isn't one of them. Yet redemption remained possible for both Karpis and Hoover, who competed neck and neck in the "Court of Criminal Appeal." Karpis's tug-of-war with J. Edgar Hoover also shined a spotlight on a justice system that needed to look beyond prison to the active work of redemption in our society.

Of equal importance, this local-to-national story serves as a reminder that if an individual is feeling disconnected from society and wants to promote dialogue, begin an inquiry into the history of *your* place—the place where you now stand.

NOTES

Introduction

1. Storm Wallace, *Dustbowl Desperadoes: Gangsters of the Dirty '30s* (Canada: Folklore Publishing, 2003), 7–8.
2. FBI, "The FBI and the American Gangster, 1924–1938," http://www.fbi.gov/about-us/history/a-centennial-history/fbi_and_the_american_gangster_1924-1938.
3. FBI, "Barker-Karpis Gang: Bremer Kidnapping," File #5-576, part 233 of 459, 8–9, https://vault.fbi.gov/barker-karpis-gang/bremer-kidnapping/bremer-kidnapping-part-233.
4. J. Edgar Hoover with Courtney Ryley Cooper, *Persons in Hiding* (Boston: Little, Brown & Company, 1938), 52.
5. Wallace, *Dustbowl Desperadoes*, 3.
6. Ibid., 8, 10.
7. *American History Journal*, "Letters: Karpis Remembered" (December 2004), April 5, 2017, www.TheHistoryNet.com.
8. Editors of *Look*, *The Story of the FBI* (New York: E.P. Dutton & Company, 1947), 126.
9. J. Edgar Hoover, "The Influence of Crime on the American Home," Vital Speeches of the Day, presented at the Round Table Forum, under the auspices of the *New York Herald Tribune*, New York City, March 11, 1936.

10. *Dayton Daily News Archive* (blog), "New Carlisle," February 6, 2013, Wright State University Special Collections & Archives, http://www.libraries. wright.edu/special/ddn_archive/2013/02/06/new-carlisle.

11. Mark J. Price, "Public Enemy #1," *Beacon Journal*, July 11, 2005, http:// www.freerepublic.com/focus/f-news/1440710/posts?page=5.

12. FBI, "Barker-Karpis Gang: Bremer Kidnapping," File #5-576, section 190, 23.

13. Michael Esslinger, *Letters from Alcatraz* (San Francisco, CA: Ocean View Publishing, 2008), 255.

14. Alvin Karpis, *The Alvin Karpis Story* (Canada: McClelland and Stewart, 1971), 256; Bryan Burrough, *Public Enemies: America's Greatest Crime Wave and the Birth of the FBI, 1933–34* (New York: Penguin Press, 2004), 515.

15. United States Census Bureau, http://www.census.gov/geo/www/ gazetteer/files/Gaz_places_national.txt.

Chapter 1

16. Sean Robinson, *News Tribune*, "Who's Who of McNeil Island Prisoners," March 28, 2011, see http://www.bellinghamherald.com/news/local/ article22203312.html.

17. San Bruno National Archives, "Alvin Karpavicz," Criminal Case File," Social History (Leavenworth, Kansas), July 29, 1936; see also Department of Justice, "Description of Prisoner," Form Rel-2, February 27, 1958, at Leavenworth; Western Reserve Historical Society, "Fourteenth Census of the United States: 1920 Population," Topeka City, January 8, 1920, ancestrylibrary.com.

18. Karpis, *Alvin Karpis Story*, 27.

19. Ibid., 27–28.

20. San Bruno National Archives, "Alvin Karpavicz Criminal Case File," Medical Record (Leavenworth, Kansas), July 31, 1936.

21. Alvin Karpis and Robert Livesey, *On the Rock: Twenty-Five Years in Alcatraz* (New York: Beaufort Books, 1980), 3; Karpis, *Alvin Karpis Story*, 29.

22. Karpis, *Alvin Karpis Story*, 30–31; FBI, "Barker-Karpis Gang Summary," File #7-576 (November 19, 1936), 3.

23. Karpis, *Alvin Karpis Story*, 176.

24. Paul Maccabee, *St. Paul Gangster History Research Collection* (Minnesota: Minnesota Historical Society, 1996), location: 143.J.9.8F, Box 4 (Grooms, Albert). This box contains letters and transcribed interviews

between Paul Maccabee and Alvin Karpis's nephew in Topeka, Kansas, in 1993.

25. FBI, archived from the original on July 1, 2014.

26. Tim Weiner, *Enemies: A History of the FBI* (New York: Random House, 2012), 69.

27. FBI, "Barker-Karpis Gang," File #7-576, bulky box 5 of 7, *Los Angeles Herald Express* and Associated Press, "Karpis Known to Pals as 'Old Creepy,'" part of FBI file, May 2, 1936, 13, https://vault.fbi.gov/barker-karpis-gang/bremer-kidnapping/bremer-kidnapping-part-458-of%20 459/view#document/p5.

Chapter 2

28. FBI, "The Kidnapping of Edward George Bremer," IC #7-576, November 19, 1936, 1–4.

29. Ibid.

30. Ibid.

31. Karpis, *Alvin Karpis Story*, 80–81.

32. Ibid., 40; J. Edgar Hoover with Ken Jones, "The Most Vicious Gang We Ever Smashed," *Amazing Detective* 12, no. 2 (June 1957): 46.

33. Karpis and Livesey, *On the Rock*, 36.

34. Raynal Pellicer, *Mug Shots: An Archive of the Famous, Infamous, and Most Wanted* (New York: Abrams, 2009), 17. Attached as Appendix A is a profile of Karpis taken after his arrest and booking on May 2, 1936.

35. Karpis and Livesey, *On the Rock*, 36.

36. Karpis, *Alvin Karpis Story*, 40–43.

37. FBI, "Kidnapping of Edward George Bremer," IC #7-576 (Washington, D.C: November 19, 1936), 1–4.

38. Ibid.; "Alvin Francis Karpis," part 3 of 3, File #32-16384 (January–December 1932), 1–16.

39. FBI, "Kidnapping of Edward George Bremer," IC #7-576, 4.

40. Hoover and Jones, "Most Vicious Gang," 46.

41. FBI, "Kidnapping of Edward George Bremer," IC #7-576, 4.

42. Karpis, *Alvin Karpis Story*, 85–86.

43. Karpis and Livesey, *On the Rock*, 36.

44. William J. Helmer and Rick Mattix, *The Complete Public Enemy Almanac* (Nashville, TN: Cumberland House, 2007), 334.

45. Karpis, *Alvin Karpis Story*, 88–89.

46. Helmer and Mattix, *Complete Public Enemy Almanac*, 461–62.
47. FBI, "George Bremer Kidnapping," File #5-576, section 241 (November 19, 1936), 8.
48. Ibid., 10.
49. Robert Ernst, *Robbin' Banks & Killin' Cops* (n.p.: PublishAmerica, 2009), 10–12; Maccabee, *St. Paul Gangster History*, "Lawrence DeVol" Case files, 143.J.9, Box 5B–7B.

Chapter 3

50. Weiner, *Enemies*, 9.
51. FBI, "Brief History of the FBI," October 2010, http://www.fbi.gov/about-us/history/brief-history.
52. Kathleen J. Frydl, "Kidnapping and State Development in the United States," *Studies in American Political Development* 20, no. 1 (March 2006): 18–19.
53. FBI, "A Byte Out of History: How the FBI Got Its Name," March 24, 2006, https://archives.fbi.gov/archives/news/stories/2006/march/fbiname_022406.
54. Curt Gentry, *J. Edgar Hoover: The Man and the Secrets* (New York: Norton, W.W. & Company, 2001), 180–81.
55. FBI, "Byte Out of History," https://archives.fbi.gov/archives/news/stories/2005/july/j.-edgar-hoovers-official-confidential-files.
56. Larry Wack, "Inspector 'Drane' Lester Coins FBI Motto," Historical G-Men, November 24, 2014, para. 3, http://historicalgmen.squarespace.com/the-birth-of-the-fbi-motto-s.

Chapter 4

57. FBI, "The Hoover Legacy: 40 Years After," part 1, May 4, 2012, https://www.fbi.gov/news/stories/the-hoover-legacy-40-years-after.
58. Ibid.
59. Gentry, *J. Edgar Hoover*, 63.
60. Ibid., 63–65.
61. Ibid.
62. Ibid., 3; Guy Lamolinara, "J. Edgar Hoover's Brief Career at the Library of Congress," Library of Congress, http://www.loc.gov/today/pr/2012/12-008.html.

63. Gentry, *J. Edgar Hoover*, 68.

64. Ibid.

65. Cheryl Lederle, "J. Edgar Hoover: The Crimebuster and the Catalogers," Library of Congress, March 27, 2012, https://blogs.loc.gov/teachers/2012/03/j-edgar-hoover-the-crimebuster-and-the-catalogers.

66. Athan G. Theoharis and John Stuart Cox, *J. Edgar Hoover and the Great American Inquisition* (Philadelphia: Temple University Press, 1988), 102.

67. Weiner, *Enemies*, 3.

68. William W. Turner, *Hoover's FBI* (New York: Thunders Mouth Press, 1993), 68.

69. Weiner, *Enemies*, 5.

70. Ibid., 6.

71. Ibid., 3–4.

72. Anthony Summers, *Official and Confidential: The Secret Life of J. Edgar Hoover* (New York: G.P. Putnam's Sons Publishers, 1993), 225.

73. Ted Schwarz, *Shocking Stories of the Cleveland Mob* (Charleston, SC: The History Press, 2010), 208, 375, 379, 398.

74. Ibid.

75. Summers, *Official and Confidential*, 242.

76. Larry Wack, "Notes on J. Edgar Hoover," Historical G-Men, http://historicalgmen.squarespace.com/j-edgar-hollywood-distorts-t.

77. Maccabee, *St. Paul Gangster History*, location: 143.J.9.8F, Box 4 (Grooms, Albert).

78. Wack, "Notes on J. Edgar Hoover."

79. Tom Wicker, "Nobody Dares to Pick His Successor," *LIFE* 70, no. 13 (n.d.): 44.

80. Summers, *Official and Confidential*, 23–24.

81. David Johnston, "Hoover: Still a Shadow Not to Be Stepped On," *New York Times*, interview with author Curt Gentry on September 9, 1991, http://www.nytimes.com/1991/09/09/books/hoover-still-a-shadow-not-to-be-stepped-on.html.

82. Ibid.

83. Special Agent James Metcalfe's poem, "We Were the G-Men," was included in his "Portraits" column in the '50s after he left the Bureau in 1935 to become a reporter and poet. Metcalfe had become an FBI agent in 1931 and worked in the Chicago Bureau. He was a member of the Dillinger Squad working under SAC Melvin Purvis. Courtesy of Larry Wack (http://historicalgmen.squarespace.com).

84. Ken Jones, "Most Vicious Gang We Ever Smashed," *Amazing Detective Case* 12, no. 2 (June 1957): 10, 11, 46–48.

85. *Inside the FBI*, produced by WETA and Channel 4, London, 1999, VHS.

86. Richard Gid Powers, *G-Men: Hoover's FBI in American Pop Culture* (Carbondale: Southern Illinois University Press, 1983), 43.

87. Phillip Brandt George, "Americana: Of Gangsters and G-Men," *American History* 39, no. 2 (June 2004): 68; *Literary Digest* 120, "Picked Police Trained by U.S.: New Crime School of Washington" (1936).

88. Larry Wack, "FBI Firearms and the Myth of the 1934 Crime Bill," Square Space, revised June 10, 2016.

89. Brian Hunt, *G-Men, Gangsters & Gators: The FBI Flying Squad and the Deaths of Ma and Fred Barker in Florida* (n.p.: Amazon Digital Services, 2012), 9–12.

90. Ibid., 9–12.

Chapter 5

91. *Owosso Argus-Press*, June 23, 1932, 11, via Associated Press; Athan G. Theoharis, *The FBI: A Comprehensive Reference Guide* (California: Greenwood, 1998), 112.

92. Tim Mahoney, *Secret Partners: Big Tom Brown and the Barker Gang* (St. Paul: Minnesota Historical Society Press, 2013), 77.

93. FBI, "Bremer Kidnapping," File #7-576, November 19, 1936, 13–14.

94. FBI, "Latent Prints in the 1933 Hamm Kidnapping," September 8, 2003, https://archives.fbi.gov/archives/news/stories/2003/september/hamm090803.

95. Mahoney, *Secret Partners*, 80; FBI, "Bremer Kidnapping," File #7-576, November 19, 1936, 13.

96. FBI, "Bremer Kidnapping," File #7-576, November 19, 1936, 13.

97. San Bruno National Archives, "Alvin Karpavicz Criminal Case File," Parole Report (Leavenworth, Kansas), August 18, 1936.

98. FBI, "Hamm Kidnapping Summary," R.C. Coulter, July 5, 1933, section 1, 30; Mahoney, *Secret Partners*, 83.

99. J. Edgar Hoover, *Technical Laboratory: Federal Bureau of Investigation* (Washington, D.C., February 1, 1940), 1.

100. FBI, "Latent Prints in the 1933 Hamm Kidnapping," September 8, 2003.

101. District Court of the United States District of Minnesota, Third Division, indictment of the grand jury, *United States of America and the District of Minnesota v. Alvin Karpavicz, alias Alvin Karpis* (St. Paul, MN, National Archives at Kansas City, June 11, 1936), no. 6258; Karpis and Livesey, *On the Rock*, 12.

102. FBI, "Kidnapping of Edward George Bremer," File #7-576, November 19, 1936; "Memorandum for the Director (Bremer)," File #7-576-207, February 8, 1934.

103. Karpis, *Alvin Karpis Story*, 168.

104. FBI, "Memorandum," April 24, 1936, received from Maccabee's *St. Paul Gangster History Collection*, Catalog ID #09-00041741, 2.

105. Karpis, *Alvin Karpis Story*, 166.

106. FBI, "Bremer Kidnapping," File #7-576, November 19, 1936, 18–19.

107. Ibid.

108. FBI FOIA, Bremer Kidnapping Summary, 19–25.

109. Hoover and Jones, "Most Vicious Gang," 47.

110. J. Edgar Hoover, *Persons in Hiding* (Boston: Little, Brown and Company, 1938), 60–61; Lew Louderback, *The Bad Ones: Gangsters of the '30s and Their Molls* (New York: Fawcett Publications, 1968), 241.

111. FBI, "Barker-Karpis Bremer Kidnapping," November 19, 1936, 23–25.

112. Ibid.

Chapter 6

113. Karpis, *Alvin Karpis Story*, 52.

114. National Archives at San Bruno, Alvin Karpis File, "Sheriff Officer's Report," Bureau of Criminal Apprehension, State Capitol, St. Paul, Minnesota, May 3, 1932.

115. FBI, "Barker-Karpis Gang," File #7-576, section 241, 8.

116. Stanley Gerstin, with an interview with J. Edgar Hoover, "G-Men Fight Crime with Science, Says J. Edgar Hoover," *Mechanix Illustrated* (October 1938): 8, http://blog.modernmechanix.com/g-men-fight-crime-with-science-hoover-interview/7/#mmGal.

117. Edna Murray, "I Was a Karpis-Barker Gang Moll," *Startling Detective* 17, no. 99 (October 1936): 38.

Chapter 7

118. Karpis, *Alvin Karpis Story*, 107–8.
119. Ibid., 107–10.
120. FBI, "Bremer Kidnapping," part 201 of 459, 13 of 139.
121. Ibid., "Karpis-Barker Gang Summary," File #5-576, part 165 of 459, 154. This section includes Dolores Delaney's testimony to special agents.
122. Karpis, *Alvin Karpis Story*, 111.
123. FBI, "Karpis-Barker Gang Summary," File #5-576, part 194 of 459, January 22, 1936, 154–56, 161, 164.
124. FBI, "Bremer Kidnapping," IC #7-576, November 19, 1936, 35.
125. Karpis, *Alvin Karpis Story*, 113.

Chapter 8

126. Karpis, *Alvin Karpis Story*, 98–99.
127. Ibid., 174–75.
128. Sam Giancana and Scott M. Burnstein, *Family Affair: Treachery, Greed, and Betrayal in the Chicago Mafia* (New York: Penguin Publishing Group, 2010), 375.
129. Ibid.
130. Ibid.
131. FBI, "A Byte Out of History: Eliot Ness and the FBI" (January 3, 2007), https://archives.fbi.gov/archives/news/stories/2007/january/ness010307.
132. Thomas Kelly, "The Great Harvard Club Raid," *Plain Dealer Sunday Magazine* (February 4, 2001): 13–17; FBI, "Bremer Kidnapping," part 127, September 1934, 31.
133. Schwarz, *Shocking Stories*, 208, 375, 379, 398.
134. Kelly, "Great Harvard Club Raid," 13–17.
135. FBI, "Bremer Kidnapping," part 272 of 459, 76–77.
136. Ibid.; *Cleveland Plain Dealer Sunday Magazine*, "Choke Crime by Its Purse, Ness Urges, Gambling Taboo Because It Gives Gangs Revenue" (February 4, 2001).
137. FBI, "Eliot Ness File," letter, visit to Eliot Ness, Director, File #62-19816-33, May 28, 1936.
138. Ibid.
139. Helmer and Mattix, *Complete Public Enemy Almanac*, 409.

140. Karpis, *Alvin Karpis Story*, 176, 178.

141. *Cleveland News*, "Three Women Freed in Kidnapping," September 1934, newspaper articles provided by author Allan May (*Jungle Inn*) on July 12, 2017.

142. Ibid.

143. Ibid.

144. Ibid.

145. FBI, "Eliot Ness File," Memo for the Director, File #62-19816-40, May 12, 1936, 1.

146. Ibid., "Eliot Ness File," 4–5.

147. Ibid., 6–7.

148. Ibid., "Bremer Kidnapping," IC #7-576, November 19, 1936, 35–37.

149. Hoover, *Persons in Hiding*, 62; FBI, "Bremer Kidnapping," part 234 of 459, 53–56.

Chapter 9

150. FBI, "Bremer Kidnapping," IC #7-576, November 19, 1936, 25, 26, https://vault.fbi.gov/barker-karpis-gang/bremer-investigation-summary/Barker-Karpis%20Gang%20Summary%20Part%201%20of%201/view.

151. Thomas McDade, "Lake Weir Revisited," 1985, part 1 of 5. Received this memoir per Jared McDade, son of Thomas McDade, via regular mail, dated September 19, 2017.

152. Maccabee, *St. Paul Gangster History*, location: 143.J.9.5B, Box 1. Information obtained from *St. Paul Pittsburgh Press*, "Kidnaping Gang Is Betrayed by Capone Gunman," April 21, 1935.

153. Jim Adams, "The FBI Goes Calling in Florida," Baby Face Nelson's Journal, http://www.babyfacenelsonjournal.com/barker-karpis-2.html; FBI, "Killing of Fred and Kate Barker at Oklawaha, Florida, While Resisting Arrest," part 108 of 459, February 8, 1935, 27–32.

154. McDade, "Lake Weir Revisited," part 3 of 5.

155. FBI, "Killing of Fred and Kate Barker at Oklawaha, Florida, While Resisting Arrest," part 108 of 459, February 8, 1935, 27–32.

156. McDade, "Lake Weir Revisited," 4 of 5.

157. FBI, "Killing of Fred and Kate Barker," part 108 of 459, February 8, 1935, 27–32.

158. Hoover and Jones, "Most Vicious Gang," 48.

159. Larry Wack, "The Barker/Karpis Gang in General," Historical G-Men, http://historicalgmen.squarespace.com/fbi-shooting-fred-kate-ma-b.

160. FBI, "Byte Out of History," January 24, 2012, https://www.fbi.gov/news/stories/copy_of_a-byte-out-of-history.
161. Ibid., "Bremer Kidnapping," part 234 of 459, 57–58, 9.

Chapter 10

162. Maccabee, *St. Paul Gangster History*, location: 143.J.9.5B, Box 1 (Bolton, William Byron, "Monty Carter," "Hamm Kidnapping"), information obtained from Associated Press, "Bremer Will Review Story of Abduction," January 19, 1935.
163. Burroughs, *Public Enemies*, 178.
164. Karpis, *Alvin Karpis Story*, 192–94.
165. Associated Press, "Escape in Battle, Then Return in Attempt to Free Two Girl Friends," January 20, 1935, 6–7.
166. FBI, "Karpis-Barker Gang Summary," File #5-576, part 194 of 459, January 22, 1936, 180, testimony of Dolores Delaney given on January 22, 1936.
167. Karpis, *Alvin Karpis Story*, 110–14.
168. FBI, "Bremer Kidnapping," File #7-576-795, part 169 of 459, November 6, 1935, 132–36.

Chapter 11

169. *Medina Gazette*, "Gangsters Visit Medina: Leave Doctor Tied Up in Guilford Grange Hall," vol. CHL, Medina Historical Society; *New York Times*, January 22, 1935.
170. Karpis, *Alvin Karpis Story*, 195–98; Michael Burg, with the Wadsworth Area Historical Society, "With Pride & Dignity: The History of the Wadsworth Police Department," 2002.
171. Wadsworth Area Historical Society, newspaper clippings, *Los Angeles Examiner* 32, no. 42, "Karpis Frees Captive: Desperadoes Race through Ohio" (January 22, 1935).
172. Duane Blubaugh, great-grandson of Wadsworth sheriff and mayor Tommy Lucas, interview on July 29, 2017, conducted by Traci Falb at the Wadsworth Area Historical Society.

Chapter 12

173. Hoover, *Persons in Hiding*, 64.

174. Ibid., 66.

175. Helmer and Mattix, *Complete Public Enemy Almanac*, 427.

176. FBI, "Karpis-Barker Gang Summary," File #7-576, November 19, 1936, 3.

177. San Bruno National Archives, "Alvin Karpavicz Criminal Case File," letter from Trumbull County Relief Commission, Warren, Ohio to director of Social Services, Atlanta, Georgia, dated June 24, 1936.

178. Ibid., 48–49.

179. Karpis, *Alvin Karpis Story*, 198–200.

180. Ibid., 200.

181. Ibid., 202–4.

182. Ibid., 31, 206; FBI, "Karpis-Barker Gang Summary," File #7-576, 50.

183. "U.S. Postal Inspectors: The Silent Service," archived from the original dated December 1, 2007, http://web.archive.org/web/20071201185210; United States Postal Service, http://www.usps.com/postalinspectors/SilentService.htm.

184. *Plain Dealer*, "2 Identified and Jailed in Mail Holdup," April 27, 1935, 1, 6.

185. FBI, "Karpis-Barker Gang," file # 7-576, November 19, 1936, 50.

186. Ibid., 49.

Chapter 13

187. FBI, "Barker-Karpis Gang Summary," File #5-576, part 190, April 22, 1936, 25.

188. Karpis, *Alvin Karpis Story*, 15–16.

189. Ibid., 209–11; William Breuer, *J. Edgar Hoover and His G-Men* (Westport, CT: Praeger Publishers, 1995), 203.

190. Karpis, *Alvin Karpis Story*, 30–31.

191. Ibid., 114, 116.

192. FBI, "Bremer Kidnapping," part 234 of 459, 83–87.

193. *St. Paul Pioneer Press*, "Shadowed Several Days," May 8, 1936.

194. FBI, "Bremer Kidnapping," File #224 of 459, part 13 of 78. He made a two-and-a-half-page statement (his name is blacked out) to W.L. Farrell with three witnesses on April 1, 1936.

195. Ibid., "Barker-Karpis Gang: Bremer Kidnapping," File #5-576, section 190, 4.

196. Karpis, *Alvin Karpis Story*, 213–14; FBI, "Barker-Karpis Gang: Bremer Kidnapping," File #5-576, section 190, 19.

197. FBI, "Barker-Karpis Gang: Bremer Kidnapping," part 272 of 459, 9, 10.

198. Karpis, *Alvin Karpis Story*, 213.

199. FBI, "Barker-Karpis Gang: Bremer Kidnapping," File #5-576, section 190, 19, https://vault.fbi.gov/barker-karpis-gang/bremer-kidnapping/bremer-kidnapping-part-224-of%20459-.

200. Ibid., File #7-576, section 231, part 272 of 459, 147.

201. Ibid.

202. Ibid., 139–40, 174.

203. Ibid.

204. Karpis, *Alvin Karpis Story*, 213; FBI, "Bremer Kidnapping," part 272 of 459, 141–43.

205. J.C. Daschbach, "Hunt 6 Train Robbers on Ohio Roads," *Cleveland Plain Dealer*, November 8, 1935, headline.

206. Ibid.

207. Karpis, *Alvin Karpis Story*, 216.

208. Ibid., 216–18; San Bruno National Archives, "Alvin Karpavicz Criminal Case Files," Admission Summary for Fred Hunter (Leavenworth, Kansas), June 24, 1936.

209. Karpis, *Alvin Karpis Story*, 216–18; San Bruno National Archives, "Alvin Karpavicz Criminal Case Files," Admission Summary for Fred Hunter (Leavenworth, Kansas), June 24, 1936; see also Annual Report of the Postmaster General, "No Hiding for Nation's 'Public Enemy #1,'" United States Postal Service, March 1936, http://about.usps.com/publications/pub162/pub162_008.htm.

210. *Warren Tribune Chronicle*, "Authorities Spread Wide Net for 6 Train Robbers," November 8, 1935, 6.

211. Claudia Garrett, e-mail dated August 9, 2018.

212. FBI, "Bremer Kidnapping," File #5-576, part 272 of 459, May 3, 1935, 141–43.

213. Ibid., section 190, 22.

214. Ibid., part 272 of 459, May 3, 1935, 141–43.

215. FBI, "Bremer Kidnapping," File #5-576, part 272 of 459, May 3, 1935, 141–43.

Chapter 14

216. FBI, "Barker-Karpis Gang Summary," File #5-576, part 190, April 22, 1936, 19.

217. Ibid., 5.

218. FBI, "Barker-Karpis Gang Summary," section 190, 57 of 126, November 19, 1936, 5.

219. Ibid., 23–24.

220. Special Agent Thomas McDade, "Thomas McDade's Journal," prepared by Thomas L. Frields, November 1934–April 20, 1938, 270 pages. Retrieved from retired agent Larry Wack and McDade's son, Jared.

221. Burrough, *Public Enemies*, 529.

222. FBI, "George Bremer Kidnapping," File #7-576, part 210 of 459, 6–9.

223. Ibid., 10; Larry Wack, retired FBI agent, phone interview.

224. *Plain Dealer*, "Karpis Captured in New Orleans," May 2, 1936, 2.

225. Maccabee, *St. Paul Gangster Files*; J. Kevin O'Brien, Chief, Freedom of Information Privacy Acts Section, "Alvin Karpis/Death Threat Letter," Washington, D.C., Federal Bureau of Investigation, October 24, 1994.

226. *Cleveland Press*, "Jail 2 Suspects in Train Holdup," November 8, 1935, 24.

227. Burrough, *Public Enemies*, 529–30.

228. FBI, "Barker-Karpis Gang," November 19, 1936, 52; Burrough, *Public Enemies*, 528–29.

229. Hoover, *Persons in Hiding*, 66.

230. FBI, "Fingerprint Identification," http://www.fbi.gov/about-us/cjis/fingerprints_biometrics/fingerprint-overview.

231. *Plain Dealer*, "Post Office Inspectors Join Police," November 8, 1935; Burrough, *Public Enemies*, 529.

232. FBI, "Barker-Karpis Gang," November 19, 1936, 52

233. Ibid., "Bremer Kidnapping," File #5-576-48320, part 174 of 459, December 9, 1935, 44.

234. *Plain Dealer*, "Fail to Link 2 in Mail Car Robbery," November 9, 1935, 7; *Cleveland Press*, "Two Suspects Arrested in Train Holdup," November 8, 1935, 1; *Plain Dealer*, "Jailed Here as Aid in Karpis Robbery," May 1, 1936, 28; "Asks Karpis Trial Here for Robbery," May 2, 1936, front page.

235. FBI, "Karpis-Barker Gang," section 241, November 19, 1936, 52.

236. FBI, "Bremer Kidnapping," File #7-576-8377, part 177 of 459, 98.

237. Ibid., 52.

238. FBI, File #7-576, section 190, Special Agent E.J. Wynn made the report at Cleveland, Ohio, April 22, 1936, 1.

239. Ibid., Affidavit of Clayton Hall, Youngtown, Ohio, April 1, 1936, 11.

240. FBI, "Bremer Kidnapping," section 190, 20; Karpis, *Alvin Karpis Story*, 222; *Cleveland Plain Dealer*, "Jailed Here as Aid," 28.

241. Wallace, *Dustbowl Desperadoes*, 134; *New York Times*, "Cummings Offers $5,000 Reward for Tip that Will Lead to the Arrest of Alvin Karpis," April 23, 1936, 1; *Cleveland Plain Dealer*, "Jailed Here as Aid," 28; *Plain Dealer*, "Freed Helps Pick Karpis Trial Site," May 3, 1936, 14.

242. FBI, "Kidnapping of Edward George Bremer, Karpis Gangster Gets One Hour for Holdup Role," part 429 of 459, 4.

243. FBI, "Bremer Kidnapping," part 234 of 459, May 3, 1935, 83–87, 90–95.

244. FBI, File #5-576, section 190, 3.

245. Ibid., 7, 9.

246. FBI, "Bremer Kidnapping," section 190, 3; W.D. Smith, *The Barker-Karpis Gang: An American Crime Family* (Tennessee: Amazon Digital Services, 2016), 285–86.

247. David Anderson, ed., *Downtown: A History of Downtown Minneapolis and Saint Paul in the Words of the People Who Lived It*, 1st ed. (Minneapolis, MN: Nodin Press, 2000), 287, 289.

248. FBI, "Karpis-Barker Gang," November 19, 1936, revised April 1984, 11.

249. Claire Bond Potter, *War on Crime: Bandits, G-Men, and the Politics of Mass Culture* (New Brunswick, NJ: Rutgers University Press, 1998), 189.

Chapter 15

250. *Newsweek* 7, no. 13, "G-Men: Senator Says They Hunt Not Only Gangsters but Glory" (May 2, 1936).

251. Francis Biddle, *In Brief Authority* (New York: Doubleday, 1967), 263–64.

252. J. Edgar Hoover testimony, Senate Appropriations Subcommittee, April 11, 1936; Burrough, *Public Enemies*, 536; Richard Gid Powers, *The Life of J. Edgar Hoover: Secrecy and Power* (New York: Free Press, 1988), 535–36; Gentry, *J. Edgar Hoover*, 185.

253. Hoover testimony, Senate Appropriations Subcommittee; De Toledano, *Hoover*, 132; Gentry, *J. Edgar Hoover*, 182–87.

254. Karpis, *Alvin Karpis Story*, 225.

255. J. Edgar Hoover with Courtney Ryley Cooper, "The Boy Who Wanted to Go Fishing," *American Magazine* 122, no. 5 (November 1936): 54–55.

256. FBI, "Bremer Kidnapping," section 190, 13; Burrough, *Public Enemies*, 534, 536.

257. Burrough, *Public Enemies*, 537.

258. FBI, "Bremer Kidnapping," part 234 of 459, May 3, 1935, 83–87, 90–95.

259. Ibid., "Alvin Karpis Summary," File #32-16384, section 1, part 2 of 3, 20–22.

260. Karpis, *Alvin Karpis Story*, 226.

261. FBI agent E.J. Connolley, "Memorandum," Federal Bureau of Investigation, May 18, 1936.

Chapter 16

262. FBI, "Bremer Kidnapping," File #7-576-11665, part 225, May 18, 1936, report by Agent Earl J. Connelley.

263. *New Castle News*, May 14, 1936, 4, Newspaper Archive, https://newspaperarchive.com/new-castle-news-may-14-1936-p-4; Hoover, "Dirty Yellow Rat," 21.

264. Agent Connelley, "Memorandum"; T.D. Quinn, Special Agent, "Memorandum of Karpis Capture," United States Federal Bureau of Investigation, May 2, 1936; Karpis and Livesey, *On the Rock*, 7.

265. Liz Scott, "The Karpis Caper When the G-Men Nabbed Their Man," *New Orleans Magazine* 32, no. 9 (June 1998): 20.

266. Hoover, "Dirty Yellow Rat," 21.

267. Karpis and Livesey, *On the Rock*, 5–6; FBI, "Alvin Karpis Summary," May 18, 1936, 8.

268. Karpis, *Alvin Karpis Story*, 27; Karpis and Livesey, *On the Rock*, 6; Larry Wack, retired FBI agent, phone interview, October 9, 2012.

269. Hoover, *Persons in Hiding*, 143; Stephen M. Underhill, "J. Edgar Hoover's Domestic Propaganda: Narrating the Spectacle of the Karpis Arrest," *Western Journal of Communication* 76, no. 4 (July–September 2012): 449.

270. Larry Wack, "Faded Glory," Historical G-Men, http://historicalgmen.squarespace.com/alvin-karpis-arrest-where-was.

271. Hoover and Jones, "Most Vicious Gang," 48.

272. Hoover, "Dirty Yellow Rat," 21; *(Toledo, OH) Times*, "Bloodless Capture," May 3, 1936; J. Edgar Hoover's Scrapbooks, Record Group 65, entry 49, Box 167, National Archives, College Park, Maryland.

273. FBI, "Kidnapping of Edward George Bremer," part 429 of 459, 6 of 92.

274. Ibid.

275. Quinn, "Memorandum"; U.S. Penitentiary–Leavenworth, Kansas, "Admission Summary: Re Alvin Karpaviez," Prison Register no. 49368-L, *Neuropsychiatric Report*, 4B, August 5, 1936, 2; Karpis and Livesey, *On the Rock*, 7; Max Allan Collins and George Hagenauer, *True Crime*, vol. 1, *G-Men and Gangsters: From Slum Gangs to the Mafia* (Forestville, CA: Eclipse Books, 1993), 47; *Washington Post*, "Karpis, '30s Gangster Freed After 32 Years," January 15, 1969, J1; *New York Times*, "Karpis Captured in New Orleans by Hoover Himself," May 2, 1936, front page.

276. Karpis and Livesey, *On the Rock*, 7; Scott, "Karpis Caper," 20; Burrough, *Public Enemies*, 540.

277. Wack, "Faded Glory."

278. Gentry, *J. Edgar Hoover*, 194.

279. Larry Wack, e-mail dated March 6, 2018, excerpt taken from the *Tribune* front-page headline).

280. *New York Times*, "Karpis Captured in New Orleans," front page.

281. Ibid., 1; *Washington Post*, "Karpis, '30s Gangster Freed," 7.

282. Burrough, *Public Enemies*, 541.

283. Hoover, *Persons in Hiding*, 27.

284. *Akron Beacon Journal*, "Desperado Is Weary, Sullen After Plane Trip from South with Hoover," May 2, 1936, 1.

285. Underhill, "J. Edgar Hoover's Domestic Propaganda," 440.

286. Bill Friedman, *All Against the Law: The Criminal Activities of the Depression-Era Bank Robbers, Mafia, FBI, Politicians, and Cops* (n.p.: Old School Histories, 2013).

287. FBI, "George Bremer Kidnapping," File #7-30, part 429, May 15, 1936, 2–10.

288. Kenneth Dickson, "In Toledo, J. Edgar Hoover Nabs No. 1 Criminal on FBI's List," *Toledo Blade*, December 17, 2008.

289. *St. Paul Dispatch*, "In Suicide Cell (Karpis)," May 8, 1936.

290. Breuer, *J. Edgar Hoover and His G-Men*, 207.

291. Gentry, *J. Edgar Hoover*, 244.

292. Richard Gid Powers, *Broken: The Troubled Past and Uncertain Future of the FBI* (New York: Free Press, 2004), 167.

293. Don Whitehead, with a foreword by J. Edgar Hoover, *The FBI Story* (New York: Simon and Schuster, 1959), 109–10.

Chapter 17

294. Maccabee, *St. Paul 1930s Gangster Research*, location 143.J.9.5B, Box 1 (Campbell, Harry "Limpy"), see FBI documents "George Bremer Kidnapping," File #5-576-11617, report dated May 15, 1936 (originated in Cincinnati, Ohio), 13–14.

295. Ibid.

296. FBI, "Karpis-Barker Gang Summary," File #5-576, November 19, 1936, 12–13, 54.

297. Ibid.

298. San Bruno National Archives, "Alvin Karpavicz Criminal Case File," Admission Summary (Leavenworth, Kansas), July 31, 1936, 2.

299. Karpis and Livesey, *On the Rock*, 24–25.

300. FBI, "Barker-Karpis Gang," File #7-576, bulky box 5 of part 7, 74; *Chicago Herald and Examiner*, "Karpis 'Wife' Tells of N.Y. Marriage," May 9, 1936.

301. FBI, "Barker-Karpis Gang Summary," File #7-576, November 19, 1936, 66.

302. Ibid., File #5-576, November 19, 1936, 54, 68.

303. San Bruno National Archives, "Alvin Karpavicz Criminal Case File," letter to Senator Robert Taft from the director of the Bureau of Prisons, July 1, 1947.

304. FBI, "Special Agent-in-Charge Pieper to the Director of the FBI," File #76-9499-11, May 13, 1943, 27–30.

305. San Bruno National Archives, "Fred John Hunter Criminal Case File," Inmates Release Schedule (Leavenworth, Kansas), Form G.O. 11, February 6, 1953.

306. Helmer and Mattix, *Complete Public Enemy Almanac*, 448.

307. Ibid., 447; San Bruno National Archives, "Fred John Hunter Criminal Case File," Monthly Report—Conditional Release, Parole Form No. 24a, June–August 1960.

Chapter 18

308. Karpis and Livesey, *On the Rock*, 15.

309. Ibid.

310. George DeVincenzi, telephone conversation/interview, November 12, 2017.

311. Karpis and Livesey, *On the Rock*, 16.
312. Associated Press, "Karpis Smiles on Board Train," August 5, 1936, 2.
313. Karpis, *Alvin Karpis Story*, 29–30.
314. *Alcatraz Examiner*, December 1959, received this article and photos by mail from former inmate Robert Schibline on August 8, 2017.
315. Karpis and Livesey, *On the Rock*, 53.
316. From David Ward, author of *Alcatraz: The Gangster Years* (2009). Ward interviewed ex-cons of Alcatraz. He mailed me these interviews with William Radkay on May 10, 2018.
317. William Radkay, *A Devil Incarnate: The Autobiography of William Radkay, #666AZ as Told to Patty Terry* (Leawood, KS: Leathers Publishing, 2005), 180.
318. FBI, "Arthur R. Doc Barker," part 2 of 2, File #76-4175-24, 23–24; David A. Ward, *Alcatraz: The Gangster Years* (Berkeley: University of California Press, 2009), 169, 487; Breuer, *J. Edgar Hoover and His G-Men*, 235.
319. Karpis and Livesey, *On the Rock*, 34, 35, 37.
320. Ibid., 50–51.
321. David Harris, "Tales from the Big House: Al Capone and Other Alcatraz Cons," *Rolling Stone* (December 20, 1973), https://www.rollingstone.com/culture/features/tales-from-the-big-house-19731220.
322. Ibid.
323. Alcatraz History, OceanView Publishing, 2018, http://www.alcatrazhistory.com/karpis.htm.
324. From Ward, who interviewed former inmate Morton Sobell (AZ-996) and mailed this interview to me on May 10, 2018.
325. Ward, *Alcatraz*, 370.
326. San Bruno National Archives, "Alvin Karpavicz Criminal Case File," Conduct Report (Alcatraz Island), report began on April 23, 1937.
327. Ibid., Special Progress Report (Alcatraz Island), Form No. 2, October 12, 1945.
328. DeVincenzi, interview, November 12, 2017.
329. Ibid.
330. Jim Albright, former Alcatraz guard, telephone interview, August 25, 2017.
331. Ibid.
332. Robert Luke, *Entombed in Alcatraz: An Autobiography by Robert Luke #1118AZ* (California: self-published, 2011), 55.
333. Bob Schibline, former Alcatraz inmate #1355, e-mail dated August 9, 2017.

334. Robert Luke, *Entombed in Alcatraz*, 9, 107–8.

335. William "Bill" Baker, former Alcatraz inmate #1259, telephone interview, February 12, 2018.

336. Milton Daniel Beacher, MD, *Alcatraz Island: Memoirs of a Rock Doc* (Lebanon, NJ: Pelican Island Publishing, n.d.), 2.

337. Ibid., 92, 194.

338. George H. Gregory, *Alcatraz Screw: My Years as a Guard in America's Most Notorious Prison* (Columbia: University of Missouri Press, 2002), 124, 185.

339. Radkay, *Devil Incarnate*, 180–81.

340. From Ward, who interviewed William Radkay in 1981 about his experiences at Alcatraz and Karpis. Ward mailed the copy of the interview on May 10, 2018, interview page 30.

341. George DeVincenzi, *Murders on Alcatraz* (San Francisco, CA: The Rock, 2014), 84.

342. Jim Albright, *Last Guard Out* (San Francisco, CA: AuthorHouse, 2008), 100.

343. Gregory, *Alcatraz Screw*, 124, 185, 218, 224–26.

Chapter 19

344. Jim Quillen, *Inside Alcatraz: My Time on the Rock* (United Kingdom: Random House, 1991), 65–66.

345. DeVincenzi, *Murders on Alcatraz*, 90–91.

346. Al Capone, letter dated January 16, 1938; see also Erin Blakemore, "This Letter Tells What Al Capone Was Up to at Alcatraz," *Smithsonian*, September 26, 2016, http://www.smithsonianmag.com/smart-news/letter-tells-what-al-capone-was-alcatraz-180960578.

347. Karpis and Livesey, *On the Rock*.

348. Bureau of Prisons, "Life at the Prison," https://www.bop.gov/about/history/alcatraz.jsp.

349. FBI, "Letter from Director of the FBI to Attorney General," File #5-576-15474, February 14, 1962.

350. Ward, *Alcatraz*, 376.

351. San Bruno National Archives, "Alvin Karpavicz Criminal File," Special Progress Report (Alcatraz Island), Classification Form 2, February 18, 1955.

352. Ibid., letter from Alcatraz Warden Edwin Swope to director of the Bureau of Prisons, May 25, 1951.

353. Karpis and Livesey, *On the Rock*, 308; San Bruno National Archives, "Alvin Karpavicz Criminal Case File," Record of Court Commitment, Form No. 1, 1941; Affidavit in Felony Case, Form 1675, May 22, 1951.
354. Bureau of Prisons, "Prison Closure," https://www.bop.gov/about/history/alcatraz.jsp.
355. Robert Schibline, former inmate #1355, interview, e-mail response dated August 4, 2017.
356. Schibline, e-mail dated August 2, 2017.
357. Ibid., e-mail response dated August 4, 2017.
358. Gregory L. Wellman, *A History of Alcatraz Island: 1853–2008* (Charleston, SC: Arcadia Publishing, 2008), 83.
359. Jerry Lewis Champion, *The Fading Voices of Alcatraz* (Bloomington, IN: AuthorHouse, 2011), 109.
360. George DeVincenzi, former Alcatraz guard, telephone interview, November 12, 2017.
361. Ward, *Alcatraz*, 374; Bureau of Prisons, teletype dated September 19, 1958, to Frank Loveland, Assistant Director, BOP, from Warden Chester Looney, Leavenworth.
362. San Bruno National Archives, "Alvin Karpavicz Criminal Case File," Bureau of Prisons Report of Injury, Form No. 73, October 10, 1961, accident on Alcatraz Island Penitentiary; Karpis and Livesey, *On the Rock*, 299–300.
363. *Alcatraz Examiner*, December 1959.
364. Ibid.
365. Karpis and Livesey, *On the Rock*, 303–4.
366. History, "Alcatraz," https://www.history.com/topics/alcatraz.
367. Ibid.

Chapter 20

368. San Bruno National Archives, "Alvin Karpavicz Criminal Case File," letter from caseworker L.R. Putnam to Mrs. Albert Grooms, April 9, 1965.
369. Ibid., letter from Frank Roberts Jr., the Catholic Rehabilitation Service in Montreal.
370. Ibid., letter from Robert "Bob" Anderson to R. Meier, Warden, McNeil Penitentiary, December 4, 1968.

371. Ibid., Notice of Release and Arrival, Parole Form I-13, January 14, 1969; Ward, *Alcatraz*, 378.

372. McDade, *Grapevine Newsletter*, May 1980, 38.

373. Robert Livesey, e-mail correspondence dated March 16, 2017.

374. Lorne Harasen, former television and radio broadcaster and open-line commentator with CKCK News Radio in Regina, phone interview, August 14, 2017; Lorne Harasen, *The Harasen Line: A Broadcaster's Memoir* (Victoria, BC: Friesen Press, 2016), 31–32.

Chapter 21

375. Maccabee, *St. Paul Gangster History*, location: 143.J.9.8F, Box 4 (Grooms, Albert).

376. Ellen Poulsen, *Don't Call Us Molls* (New York: Clinton Cook Publishing Corporation, 2002), 406.

377. FBI, "Bremer Kidnapping," File #7-576-77, letters from Dolores Delaney, part 168 of 459, 174–76.

378. Ibid.

379. U.S. District Court, Southern District of Florida, *U.S. v. Dolores Delaney*, National Archives, Southeast Region, East Point Georgia; Poulsen, *Don't Call Us Molls*, 385, 405–6.

380. Maccabee, *St. Paul Gangster History* (Grooms, Albert).

381. San Bruno Archives, "Alvin Karpavicz Criminal Case File."

382. Ibid., memorandum for File from Robert J. Kaiser, Associate Warden, via parole officer, dated April 9, 1958.

383. Ibid., letter generated from the United States District Court, Office of the Probation Officer (Chicago, Illinois), to Chief D.L. Yeagley, Classification and Parole at Leavenworth Penitentiary, Kansas, re: Karpavicz, Alvin (#49368), April 14, 1958.

384. Susan Henry, phone interview, January 26, 2018. Henry is the step-granddaughter of Dee Higby (known as Dolores Delaney).

385. *Chicago Sun-Times*, obituary of Raymond A. "Creepy" Karpis, http://legacy.suntimes.com/obituaries/chicagosuntimes/obituary.aspx?page=lifestory&pid=107702.

386. *Arizona Republic*, "Dee M. Higby," April 27, 1985, 34.

Chapter 22

387. Letter from Harold Hecht to Alvin Karpis, dated October 27, 1976. This letter was e-mailed on September 13, 2017, courtesy of Jared McDade, son of former FBI agent Thomas McDade (1934–38).
388. McDade, *Grapevine Newsletter* (Spring 1978).
389. Letter from Hecht to Karpis, October 27, 1976.
390. *Hollywood Reporter*, "Paramount to Film 'Last Public Enemy,'" September 13, 1976. This article was e-mailed to me by Jared McDade on September 13, 2017.
391. Thomas M. McDade, "Biography," e-mailed by son, Jared McDade, on September 12, 2017.

Chapter 23

392. Earl Schenck Miers, *The Story of the FBI* (New York: Wonder Books, 1965), 124.
393. Ibid., 126.
394. Maccabee, *St. Paul Gangster History*, location: 143.J.9.8F, Box 4 (Grooms, Albert).
395. *Washington Post*, "Karpis, '30s Gangster Freed," 7; *Plain Dealer*, "'30s Hood Terrorized Midwest: Alvin Karpis Dies in Spain, Robbed Train in Garrettsville," August 29, 1979, 17-A. This article calls Karpis's heist the "last big train robbery in the United States."
396. Robert Livesey, "Little Brick Schoolhouse," information about Alvin Karpis re: death, http://www.littlebrick.com/alvinkarpis/about/7-death/index.html.

Final Thoughts

397. Karpis, *Alvin Karpis Story*, 210–11.
398. Ibid., 256.
399. Portage County Auditor's Office, Tax Map Department, Village of Garrettsville, H (Hiram) 45A, Ravenna, Ohio, January 2009, retrieved March 5, 2013, http://www.co.portage.oh.us/GIS/Parcel_PDFs/hiram/45a.pdf.

ABOUT THE AUTHOR

A lifelong native of Northeast Ohio, historian Julie Thompson completed her history degree at Hiram College, where she graduated with distinction. She has volunteered at the U.S. Holocaust Memorial Museum and worked extensively with the Library of Congress Publishing Office on four of its substantial published works. Julie remains an active member of the Freedom Township Historical Society and has served on the board of trustees for the James A. Garfield Historical Society, where she engaged with Hiram College to develop the society's first internship program and served as a member of her area's Inter-Museum Council.

Visit us at
www.historypress.com